WORLD

WATCH

COLLINS WORLD WATCH
Collins
An Imprint of HarperCollins Publishers
Westerhill Road
Bishopbriggs
Glasgow
G64 2QT

© HarperCollins Publishers 2012
Maps © Collins Bartholomew Ltd 2012

First published 2010
Second edition 2012
ISBN 978-0-00-748822-3

The contents of this edition of Collins World
Watch are believed correct at the time of printing.
Nevertheless the publishers can accept no
responsibility for errors or omissions, changes in
the detail given, or for any expense or loss thereby
caused.

British Library Cataloguing in Publication Data
A catalogue record for this book is available from the
British Library

Printed and bound in Hong Kong.

Design © HarperCollins Publishers

World Development Indicator Data supplied by the
World Bank.
The findings, interpretations, and conclusions
expressed here are those of the author(s) and do
not necessarily reflect the views of the Board of
Executive Directors of the International Bank for
Reconstruction and Development / World Bank or
the governments they represent. The World Bank
does not guarantee the accuracy of the data included
in this work. The boundaries, colours, denominations,
and other information shown on any map in this
work do not imply on the part of the World Bank any
judgment of the legal status of any territory or the
endorsement or acceptance of such boundaries.

All mapping in this atlas is generated from Collins
Bartholomew digital databases.
Collins Bartholomew, the UK's leading independent
geographical information supplier, can provide a
digital, custom, and premium mapping service to a
variety of markets.
For further information: Tel: +44 (0) 208 307 4515
e-mail: collinsbartholomew@harpercollins.co.uk
Visit our websites at:
www.collinseducation.com
www.collinsbartholomew.com

WORLD

A DYNAMIC VISUAL GUIDE PACKED
WITH FASCINATING FACTS ABOUT THE WORLD

WATCH

Collins

Contents

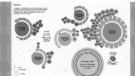

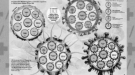

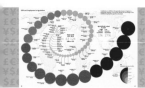

Urban Population–16

Life Expectancy–18

Ageing Population–20

Dependent Population–22

Cities of the World–24

Birth and Fertility Rates–36

Maternal Health–38

Death Rates–40

Child Mortality–42

Access to Safe Water–44

ECONOMY

Economy 56-77

Agriculture–58

Income–60

Most Visited Countries–62

Economic Growth–64

Aid Donors and Receivers–76

ENVIRONMENT

Environment 78-109

Environment and Development–80

Physical World–82

Biomes of the World–84

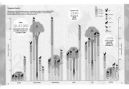
Threatened Species–96

Animal Survival–98

Energy Use–100

Primary energy consumption–102

Global Warming–104

Millennium Development Goals Achievement Fund–118

World Statistics–120

Definitions–136

Notes, Index & Acknowledgements–140

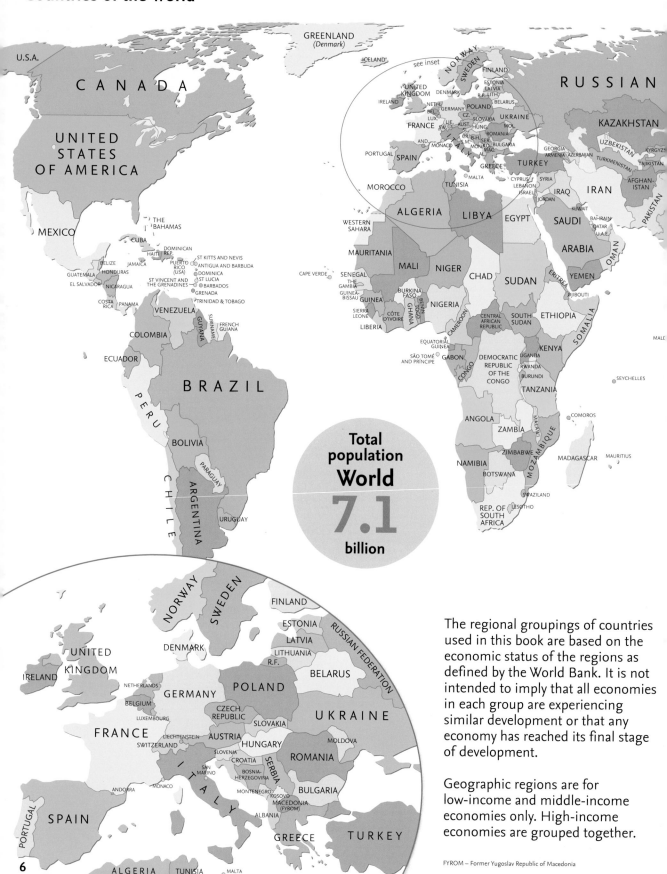

Total population World 7.1 billion

The regional groupings of countries used in this book are based on the economic status of the regions as defined by the World Bank. It is not intended to imply that all economies in each group are experiencing similar development or that any economy has reached its final stage of development.

Geographic regions are for low-income and middle-income economies only. High-income economies are grouped together.

FYROM – Former Yugoslav Republic of Macedonia

DERATION

MONGOLIA

CHINA

NORTH KOREA

SOUTH KOREA

JAPAN

VIETNAM

NEPAL

BHUTAN

BANGLA-DESH

IA

MYANMAR (BURMA)

THAILAND

CAMBODIA

PHILIPPINES

SRI LANKA

BRUNEI

MALAYSIA

SINGAPORE

INDONESIA

PALAU

FED. STATES OF MICRONESIA

MARSHALL ISLANDS

KIRIBATI

NAURU

PAPUA NEW GUINEA

SOLOMON ISLANDS

EAST TIMOR

TUVALU

SAMOA

VANUATU

FIJI

TONGA

AUSTRALIA

NEW ZEALAND

Highest population China 1.3 billion

Economic regions

East Asia & Pacific

American Samoa	Marshall Islands	Samoa
Cambodia	Micronesia,	Solomon Islands
China	Federated States of	Thailand
East Timor	Mongolia	Tonga
Fiji	Myanmar	Tuvalu
Indonesia	North Korea	Vanuatu
Kiribati	Palau	Vietnam
Laos	Papua New Guinea	
Malaysia	Philippines	

Europe & Central Asia

Albania	Kosovo	Russian Federation
Armenia	Kyrgyzstan	Serbia
Azerbaijan	Latvia	Tajikistan
Belarus	Lithuania	Turkey
Bosnia-Herzegovina	Macedonia (FYROM)	Turkmenistan
Bulgaria	Moldova	Ukraine
Georgia	Montenegro	Uzbekistan
Kazakhstan	Romania	

High-income

Andorra	Greece	Portugal
Antigua & Barbuda	Greenland	Qatar
Australia	Hungary	San Marino
Austria	Iceland	Saudi Arabia
Bahamas, The	Ireland	Singapore
Bahrain	Israel	Slovakia
Barbados	Italy	Slovenia
Belgium	Japan	South Korea
Brunei	Kuwait	Spain
Canada	Liechtenstein	Sweden
Croatia	Luxembourg	Switzerland
Cyprus	Malta	United Kingdom
Czech Republic	Monaco	United States of
Denmark	Netherlands	America
Equatorial Guinea	New Zealand	Trinidad & Tobago
Estonia	Norway	United Arab
Finland	Oman	Emirates
France	Poland	
Germany	Puerto Rico	

Latin America & Caribbean

Antigua & Barbuda	Ecuador	Paraguay
Argentina	El Salvador	Peru
Belize	Grenada	St. Kitts and Nevis
Bolivia	Guatemala	St. Lucia
Brazil	Guyana	St. Vincent and the
Chile	Haiti	Grenadines
Colombia	Honduras	Suriname
Costa Rica	Jamaica	Uruguay
Cuba	Mexico	Venezuela
Dominica	Nicaragua	
Dominican Republic	Panama	

Middle East & North Africa

Algeria	Jordan	Tunisia
Djibouti	Lebanon	West Bank and Gaza
Egypt	Libya	Yemen
Iran	Morocco	
Iraq	Syria	

South Asia

Afghanistan	India	Pakistan
Bangladesh	Maldives	Sri Lanka
Bhutan	Nepal	

Sub-Saharan Africa

Angola	Gabon	Rwanda
Benin	Gambia, The	São Tomé and
Botswana	Ghana	Príncipe
Burkina Faso	Guinea	Senegal
Burundi	Guinea-Bissau	Seychelles
Cameroon	Kenya	Sierra Leone
Cape Verde	Lesotho	Somalia
Central African	Liberia	South Africa
Republic	Madagascar	South Sudan
Chad	Malawi	Sudan
Comoros	Mali	Swaziland
Congo	Mauritania	Tanzania
Congo, Democratic	Mauritius	Togo
Republic of the	Mozambique	Uganda
Côte d'Ivoire	Namibia	Zambia
Eritrea	Niger	Zimbabwe
Ethiopia	Nigeria	

Economic regions

East Asia & Pacific	Middle East & North Africa
Europe & Central Asia	South Asia
High-income	Sub-Saharan Africa
Latin America & Caribbean	no data

Regional Groupings

The regional groupings, of countries, used on this map are based on the per capita income of each country. Economies are divided according to Gross National Income per capita and classified as low income, middle income (subdivided into lower middle and upper middle), or high income. Classification by income does not necessarily reflect development status.

North America

- Bermuda
- Canada
- United States

Europe & Central Asia

- Andorra
- Austria
- Belgium
- Croatia
- Cyprus
- Czech Republic
- Denmark
- Estonia
- Finland
- France
- Germany
- Greece
- Hungary
- Iceland
- Ireland

- Italy
- Liechtenstein
- Luxembourg
- Monaco
- Netherlands
- Norway
- Poland
- Portugal
- San Marino
- Slovakia
- Slovenia
- Spain
- Sweden
- Switzerland
- United Kingdom

- Albania
- Azerbaijan
- Belarus
- Bosnia and Herzegovina
- Bulgaria
- Kazakhstan
- Latvia
- Lithuania
- Macedonia
- Montenegro
- Romania
- Rus. Federation
- Serbia
- Turkey

- Armenia
- Georgia
- Kosovo
- Moldova
- Turkmenistan
- Ukraine
- Uzbekistan

- Kyrgyzstan
- Tajikistan

Latin America & Caribbean

- The Bahamas
- Barbados
- Puerto Rico
- Trinidad and Tobago

- Antigua and Barbuda
- Argentina
- Brazil
- Chile
- Colombia
- Costa Rica
- Cuba
- Dominica
- Dominican Rep.
- Ecuador
- Grenada
- Jamaica
- Mexico
- Panama
- Peru
- St. Kitts and Nevis
- St. Lucia
- St. Vincent & the Grenadines
- Suriname
- Uruguay
- Venezuela

- Belize
- Bolivia
- El Salvador
- Guatemala
- Guyana
- Honduras
- Nicaragua
- Paraguay

- Haiti

Sub-Saharan Africa

- Equatorial Guinea

- Botswana
- Gabon
- Mauritius
- Mayotte
- Namibia
- Seychelles
- South Africa

- Angola
- Cameroon
- Cape Verde
- Congo
- Cote d'Ivoire
- Ghana
- Lesotho
- Mauritania
- Nigeria
- Sao Tome & Principe
- Senegal
- Sudan
- Swaziland
- Zambia

- Benin
- Burkina Faso
- Burundi
- Central African Rep.
- Chad
- Comoros
- Dem. Rep. of the Congo
- Eritrea
- Ethiopia
- The Gambia
- Guinea
- Guinea-Bissau
- Kenya

- Liberia
- Madagascar
- Malawi
- Mali
- Mozambique
- Niger
- Rwanda
- Sierra Leone
- Somalia
- Tanzania
- Togo
- Uganda
- Zimbabwe

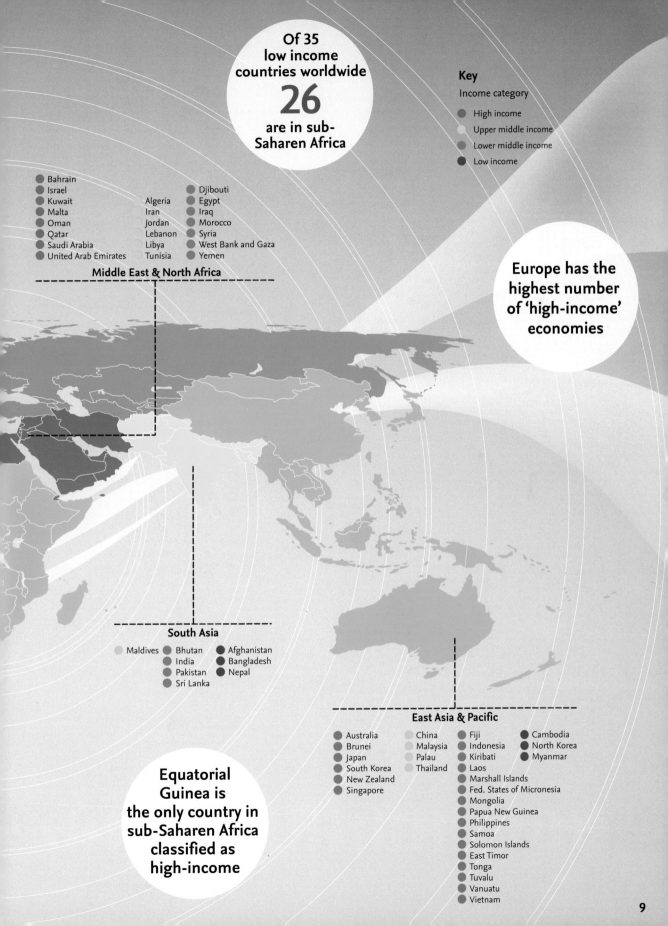

Of 35
low income
countries worldwide
26
are in sub-
Saharen Africa

Key
Income category
- High income
- Upper middle income
- Lower middle income
- Low income

Middle East & North Africa

- Bahrain
- Israel
- Kuwait
- Malta
- Oman
- Qatar
- Saudi Arabia
- United Arab Emirates

- Algeria
- Iran
- Jordan
- Lebanon
- Libya
- Tunisia

- Djibouti
- Egypt
- Iraq
- Morocco
- Syria
- West Bank and Gaza
- Yemen

**Europe has the
highest number
of 'high-income'
economies**

South Asia

- Maldives
- India
- Pakistan
- Sri Lanka

- Bhutan

- Afghanistan
- Bangladesh
- Nepal

**Equatorial
Guinea is
the only country in
sub-Saharen Africa
classified as
high-income**

East Asia & Pacific

- Australia
- Brunei
- Japan
- South Korea
- New Zealand
- Singapore

- China
- Malaysia
- Palau
- Thailand

- Fiji
- Indonesia
- Kiribati
- Laos
- Marshall Islands
- Fed. States of Micronesia
- Mongolia
- Papua New Guinea
- Philippines
- Samoa
- Solomon Islands
- East Timor
- Tonga
- Tuvalu
- Vanuatu
- Vietnam

- Cambodia
- North Korea
- Myanmar

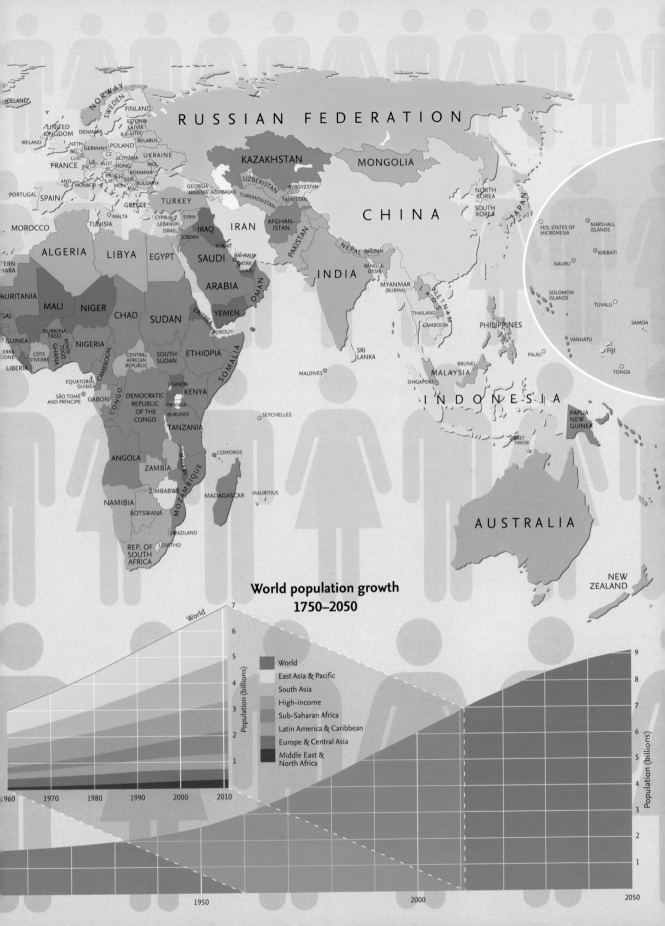

World population growth 1750–2050

Urban Population

Cities, now home to almost half of the world's population, are growing rapidly in size and number, especially in developing countries. People flock to cities for work, access to public services, and a higher standard of living. Cities can be tremendously efficient, as it is easier to provide water and sanitation services to people living together in urban settings than in dispersed rural communities. The cost of meeting basic needs increases as cities grow, as does the demand on the environment and natural resources.

51% of the world's population lives in towns and cities

Urban attractions

- Good medical care
- Available housing and services
- Good educational facilities
- Transport network
- Medical facilities
- Job opportunities

Key

Urban population (% per country)

- 90 – 100
- 75 – 89.9
- 60 – 74.9
- 49.9 – 59.9
- 30 – 49.8
- 0 – 29.9
- no data

Village in rural Mali

Urban population by region 1960–2010 (million people)

- East Asia & Pacific
- High-income
- South Asia
- Latin America & Caribbean
- Sub-Saharan Africa
- Europe & Central Asia
- Middle East & North Africa

1960   1965   1970   1975   1980

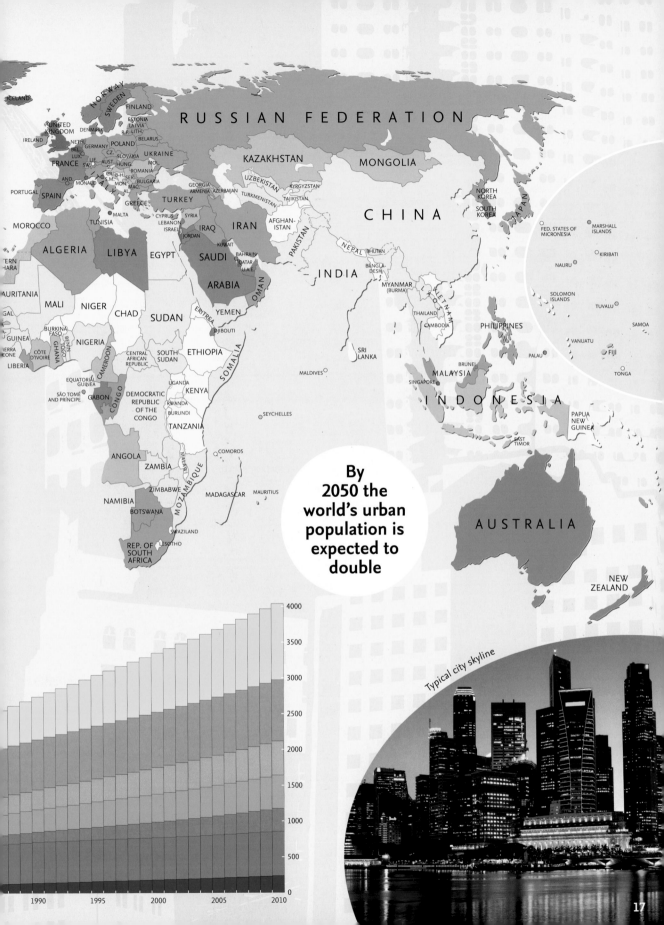

RUSSIAN FEDERATION

ICELAND
NORWAY
SWEDEN
FINLAND
UNITED KINGDOM
IRELAND
DENMARK
ESTONIA
LATVIA
R.F. LITH.
BELARUS
NETH.
BEL.
LUX.
GERMANY
POLAND
KAZAKHSTAN
MONGOLIA
FRANCE
CZ
SLOVAKIA
AUST.
HUNG.
UKRAINE
AND.
LIE.
SW.
S.M.
SER.
MOL.
ROMANIA
BULGARIA
UZBEKISTAN
KYRGYZSTAN
PORTUGAL
SPAIN
MONACO
ITALY
GREECE
TURKEY
GEORGIA
ARMENIA
AZERBAIJAN
TURKMENISTAN
TAJIKISTAN
NORTH KOREA
SOUTH KOREA
JAPAN
MALTA
CYPRUS
LEBANON
ISRAEL
SYRIA
IRAQ
JORDAN
IRAN
AFGHAN-ISTAN
CHINA
FED. STATES OF MICRONESIA
MARSHALL ISLANDS
MOROCCO
TUNISIA
KUWAIT
BAHRAIN
QATAR
U.A.E.
SAUDI ARABIA
PAKISTAN
NEPAL
BHUTAN
NAURU
KIRIBATI
ALGERIA
LIBYA
EGYPT
OMAN
INDIA
BANGLA-DESH
MYANMAR (BURMA)
SOLOMON ISLANDS
TUVALU
SAMOA
ERN HARA
MAURITANIA
MALI
NIGER
CHAD
SUDAN
ERITREA
YEMEN
LAOS
THAILAND
VIETNAM
PHILIPPINES
VANUATU
FIJI
GAL
GUINEA
BURKINA FASO
NIGERIA
DJIBOUTI
ETHIOPIA
CAMBODIA
PALAU
TONGA
IERRA EONE
CÔTE D'IVOIRE
BENIN
TOGO
GHANA
CENTRAL AFRICAN REPUBLIC
SOUTH SUDAN
SOMALIA
SRI LANKA
BRUNEI
MALAYSIA
LIBERIA
EQUATORIAL GUINEA
CAMEROON
UGANDA
KENYA
MALDIVES
SINGAPORE
SÃO TOMÉ AND PRÍNCIPE
GABON
CONGO
DEMOCRATIC REPUBLIC OF THE CONGO
RWANDA
BURUNDI
TANZANIA
SEYCHELLES
INDONESIA
PAPUA NEW GUINEA
ANGOLA
ZAMBIA
MALAWI
COMOROS
EAST TIMOR
NAMIBIA
ZIMBABWE
MOZAMBIQUE
MADAGASCAR
MAURITIUS
BOTSWANA
AUSTRALIA
SWAZILAND
REP. OF SOUTH AFRICA
LESOTHO
NEW ZEALAND

By 2050 the world's urban population is expected to double

Typical city skyline

1990   1995   2000   2005   2010

4000
3500
3000
2500
2000
1500
1000
500
0

Life Expectancy

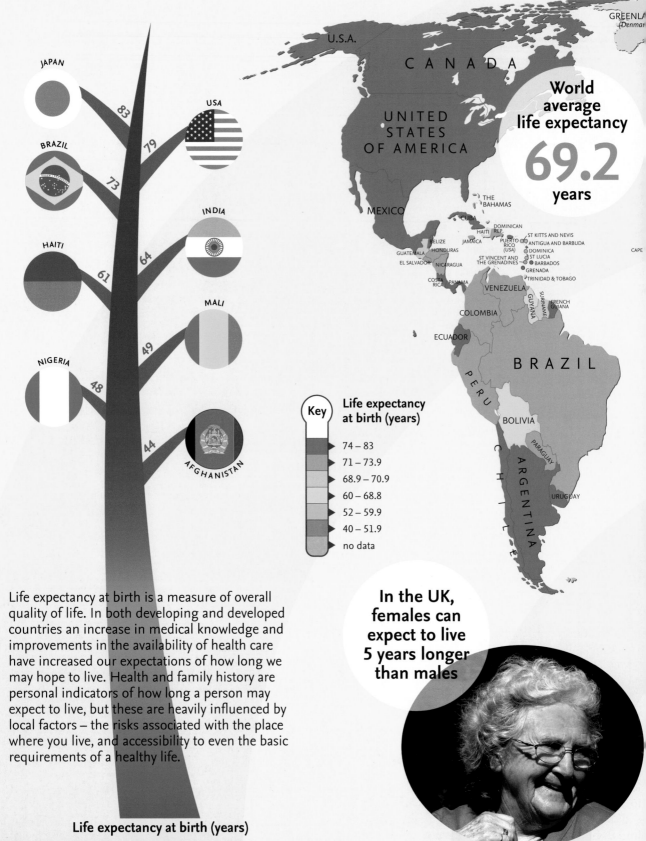

JAPAN **83**

USA **79**

BRAZIL **73**

INDIA **64**

HAITI **61**

MALI **49**

NIGERIA **48**

AFGHANISTAN **44**

Life expectancy at birth (years)

U.S.A.

C A N A D A

GREENLAND (Denmark)

UNITED STATES OF AMERICA

World average life expectancy

69.2

years

MEXICO

THE BAHAMAS

CUBA

HAITI DOMINICAN REP.

ST KITTS AND NEVIS

BELIZE

JAMAICA

PUERTO RICO (USA)

ANTIGUA AND BARBUDA

GUATEMALA

HONDURAS

DOMINICA

ST LUCIA

EL SALVADOR

NICARAGUA

ST VINCENT AND THE GRENADINES

BARBADOS

CAPE

GRENADA

COSTA RICA

PANAMA

TRINIDAD & TOBAGO

VENEZUELA

GUYANA

SURINAME

FRENCH GUIANA

COLOMBIA

ECUADOR

B R A Z I L

P E R U

BOLIVIA

PARAGUAY

C H I L E

A R G E N T I N A

URUGUAY

Key — **Life expectancy at birth (years)**

- 74 – 83
- 71 – 73.9
- 68.9 – 70.9
- 60 – 68.8
- 52 – 59.9
- 40 – 51.9
- no data

Life expectancy at birth is a measure of overall quality of life. In both developing and developed countries an increase in medical knowledge and improvements in the availability of health care have increased our expectations of how long we may hope to live. Health and family history are personal indicators of how long a person may expect to live, but these are heavily influenced by local factors – the risks associated with the place where you live, and accessibility to even the basic requirements of a healthy life.

In the UK, females can expect to live 5 years longer than males

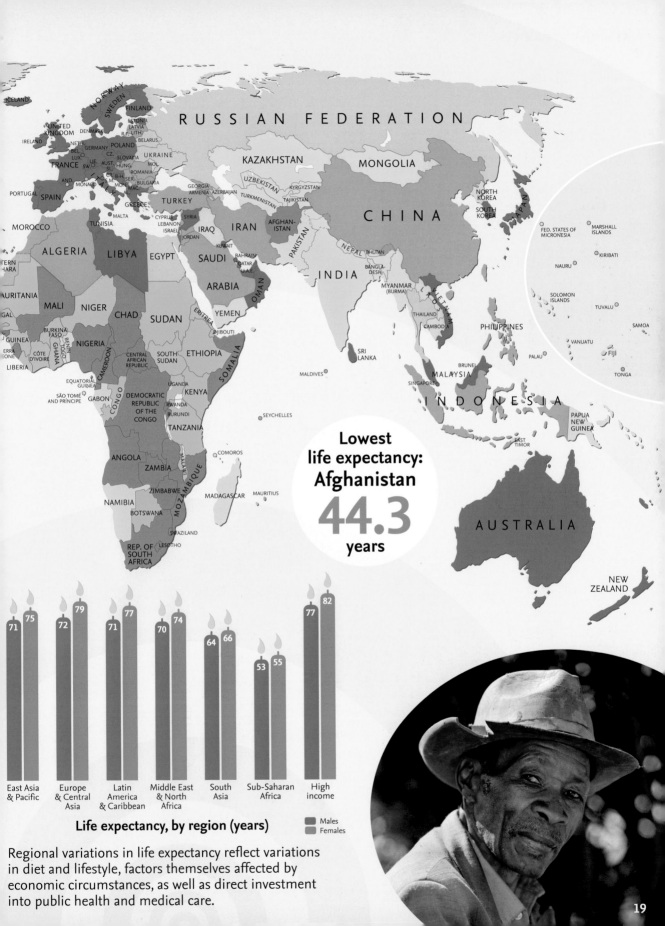

ICELAND

NORWAY SWEDEN FINLAND

UNITED KINGDOM
IRELAND
DENMARK
ESTONIA
LATVIA
R.F. LITH.
Belarus

RUSSIAN FEDERATION

FRANCE
GERMANY POLAND
NETH.
BEL.
LUX.
AND.
LIE. SW.
AUST.
HUNG.
CZ.
SLOVAKIA
SL.
B.-H.
SER.
MAC.
MON.
ROMANIA
BULGARIA
UKRAINE

KAZAKHSTAN

MONGOLIA

PORTUGAL
SPAIN
ITALY
GREECE
MALTA
CYPRUS
LEBANON
ISRAEL
TURKEY
GEORGIA
ARMENIA AZERBAIJAN
UZBEKISTAN
TURKMENISTAN
KYRGYZSTAN
TAJIKISTAN

NORTH KOREA
SOUTH KOREA
JAPAN

CHINA

MOROCCO
TUNISIA
SYRIA
IRAQ
JORDAN
IRAN
AFGHAN-ISTAN

FED. STATES OF MICRONESIA
MARSHALL ISLANDS

ALGERIA
LIBYA
EGYPT
KUWAIT
BAHRAIN
QATAR
U.A.E.
SAUDI
ARABIA
PAKISTAN
NEPAL
BHUTAN

KIRIBATI

NAURU

WESTERN SAHARA

MAURITANIA
MALI
NIGER
CHAD
SUDAN
ERITREA
DJIBOUTI
YEMEN
OMAN
INDIA
BANGLA-DESH
MYANMAR (BURMA)
LAOS
SOLOMON ISLANDS

TUVALU

SAMOA

SENEGAL
GUINEA
BURKINA FASO
NIGERIA
BENIN
TOGO
GHANA
CÔTE D'IVOIRE
SIERRA LEONE
LIBERIA
CENTRAL AFRICAN REPUBLIC
SOUTH SUDAN
ETHIOPIA
SOMALIA
THAILAND
CAMBODIA
VIETNAM
PHILIPPINES

VANUATU
FIJI
TONGA

EQUATORIAL GUINEA
SÃO TOMÉ AND PRÍNCIPE
GABON
CONGO
CAMEROON
DEMOCRATIC REPUBLIC OF THE CONGO
UGANDA
RWANDA
BURUNDI
KENYA
TANZANIA

SRI LANKA
MALDIVES
MALAYSIA
SINGAPORE
BRUNEI
PALAU

INDONESIA

SEYCHELLES

PAPUA NEW GUINEA

ANGOLA
ZAMBIA
MALAWI
MOZAMBIQUE
ZIMBABWE
NAMIBIA
BOTSWANA
SWAZILAND
REP. OF SOUTH AFRICA
LESOTHO
COMOROS
MADAGASCAR
MAURITIUS

EAST TIMOR

Lowest life expectancy: Afghanistan

44.3

years

AUSTRALIA

NEW ZEALAND

Life expectancy, by region (years)

Region	Males	Females
East Asia & Pacific	71	75
Europe & Central Asia	72	79
Latin America & Caribbean	71	77
Middle East & North Africa	70	74
South Asia	64	66
Sub-Saharan Africa	53	55
High income	77	82

■ Males
■ Females

Regional variations in life expectancy reflect variations in diet and lifestyle, factors themselves affected by economic circumstances, as well as direct investment into public health and medical care.

Ageing Population

In almost every country in the world the proportion of elderly people in the population is growing. In the industrial world there is an unprecedented increase in the proportion of the population aged over 65 and people are expecting to live longer than their ancestors could ever hope to. An ageing population is an indicator of social development and it represents the success of a country's health care policies, but it also means that there are fewer people of working age to support and care for the well-being of a growing number of dependent elderly people.

Population structure 1950–2050

Each full square represents 1% of the total population

World

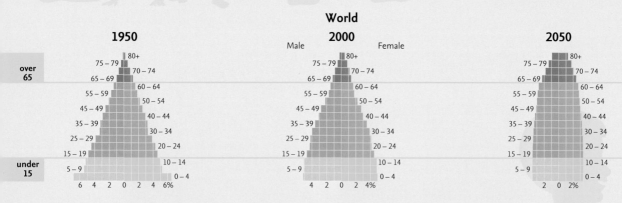

More developed regions

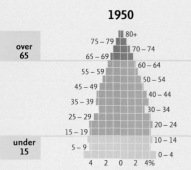
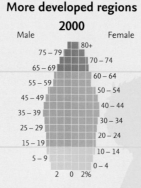
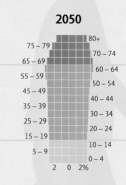

Least developed regions

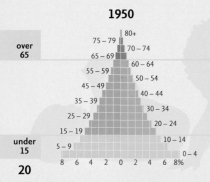
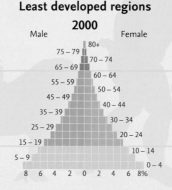

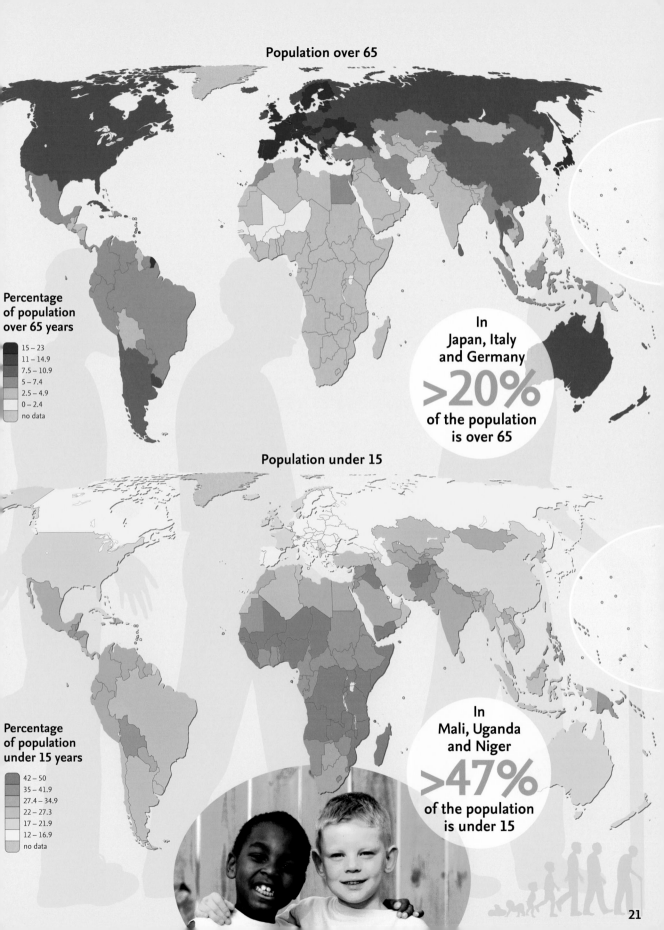

Population over 65

Percentage of population over 65 years

- 15 – 23
- 11 – 14.9
- 7.5 – 10.9
- 5 – 7.4
- 2.5 – 4.9
- 0 – 2.4
- no data

In
Japan, Italy
and Germany
>20%
of the population
is over 65

Population under 15

Percentage of population under 15 years

- 42 – 50
- 35 – 41.9
- 27.4 – 34.9
- 22 – 27.3
- 17 – 21.9
- 12 – 16.9
- no data

In
Mali, Uganda
and Niger
>47%
of the population
is under 15

21

Dependent Population

The elderly dependent population is significantly greater now than fifty years ago. This trend is expected to continue.

More Developed Regions

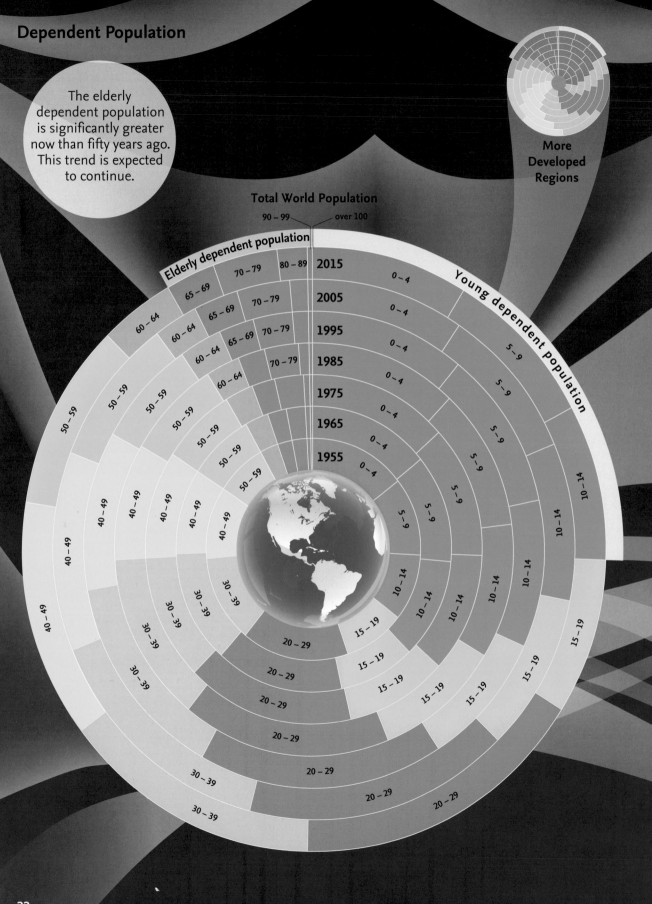

Total World Population

90 – 99   over 100

Elderly dependent population

Young dependent population

70 – 79   80 – 89   **2015**

65 – 69   70 – 79   **2005**

60 – 64   65 – 69   70 – 79   **1995**

60 – 64   65 – 69   70 – 79   **1985**

60 – 64   70 – 79   **1975**

50 – 59   60 – 64   **1965**

50 – 59   **1955**

0 – 4

5 – 9

10 – 14

15 – 19

20 – 29

30 – 39

40 – 49

50 – 59

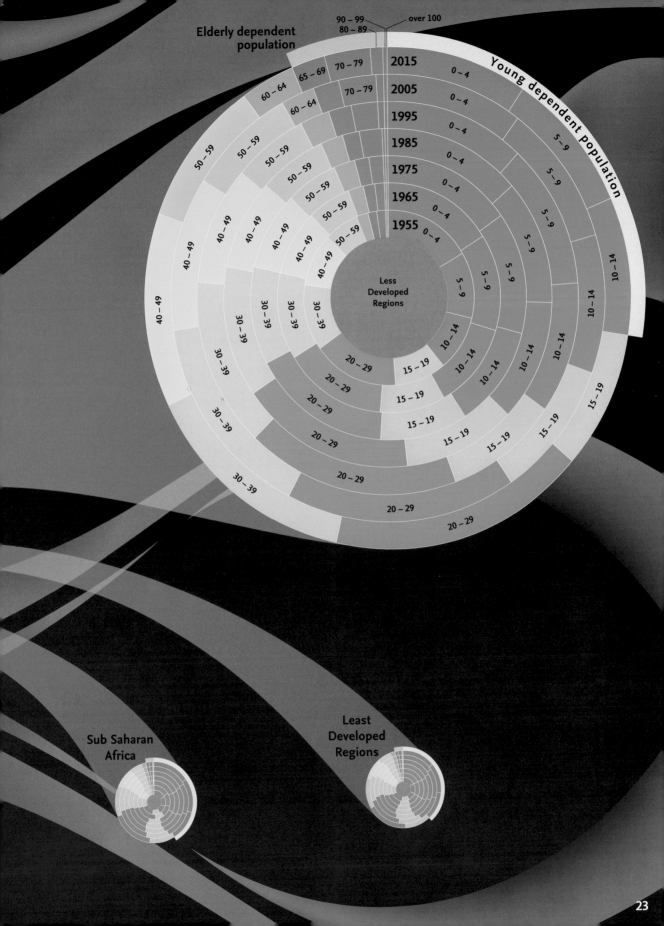

Elderly dependent population

Young dependent population

90 – 99
80 – 89
over 100

| 2015 |
| 2005 |
| 1995 |
| 1985 |
| 1975 |
| 1965 |
| 1955 |

65 – 69
70 – 79
70 – 79
60 – 64
60 – 64
60 – 64

50 – 59

40 – 49

30 – 39

20 – 29

15 – 19

10 – 14

5 – 9

0 – 4

Less
Developed
Regions

Sub Saharan
Africa

Least
Developed
Regions

23

Cities of the World

Providing the infrastructure and administration to support large concentrations of population poses a challenge to all major cities. Fast growing cities in developing countries suffer widespread poverty and poor public health but issues such as traffic congestion, water supply and pollution affect cities everywhere. World cities also play an important role in the global economy. They are often the headquarters of multinational corporations, international organizations and financial institutions. Many are capital cities wielding an economic, political and cultural influence way beyond their administrative boundaries.

Los Angeles leads the world in the creation of motion pictures, TV production, interactive games and music recording

Population (2015)

Area (sq km)

Population density (people per sq km)

Los Angeles USA

12.8 | 4320 | 2957

Over 20% of people living in New York were born outside the USA

New York

Mexico City is the largest city in North America

Mexico City

Los Angeles

New York USA

19.4 | 8683 | 2239

Mexico City Mexico

19.5 | 2072 | 9404

São Paulo has **>15** million square metres of green space

Rio de Janeiro

São Paulo

Buenos Aires

Residents in São Paulo come from 100 different ethnic backgrounds including 6 million Italians and 3 million Portuguese

São Paulo Brazil

19.6 | 1968 | 9950

City growth 1950–2050

Population (millions)

40 — 35 — 30 — 25 — 20 — 15 — 10 — 5 — 0

New York · Tokyo · London · Paris · Shanghai · Moscow · Buenos Aires · Kolkata · Beijing · Osaka · Los Angeles · Rio de Janeiro

2050
2015
2005
1950

City populations 2015

36 094 000 — Tokyo
20 072 000 — Mumbai
19 582 000 — São Paulo
19 485 000 — Mexico City
19 411 000 — New York
17 015 000 — Delhi
15 789 000 — Shanghai
15 577 000 — Kolkata
14 796 000 — Dhaka
13 089 000 — Buenos Aires

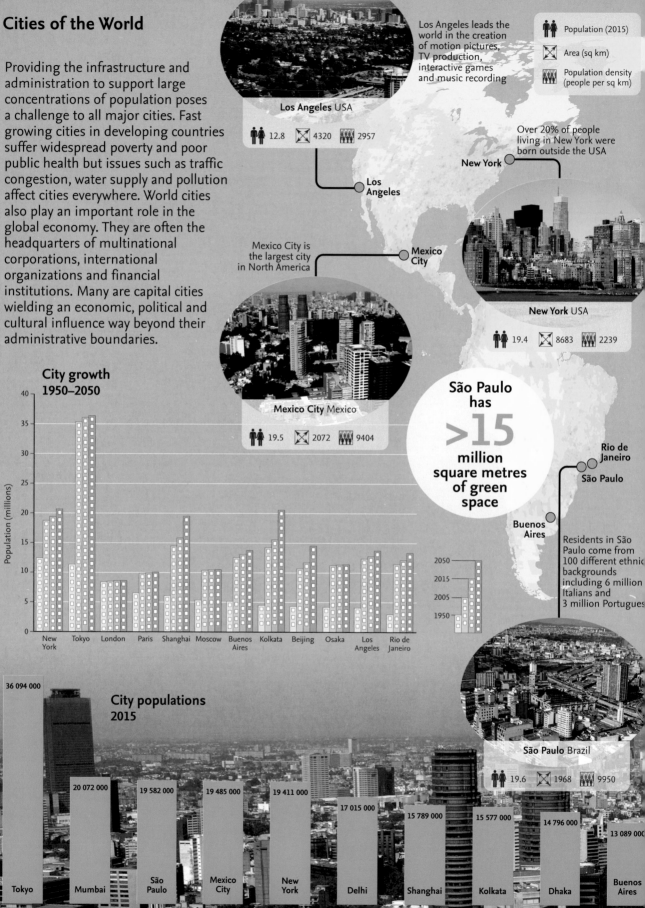

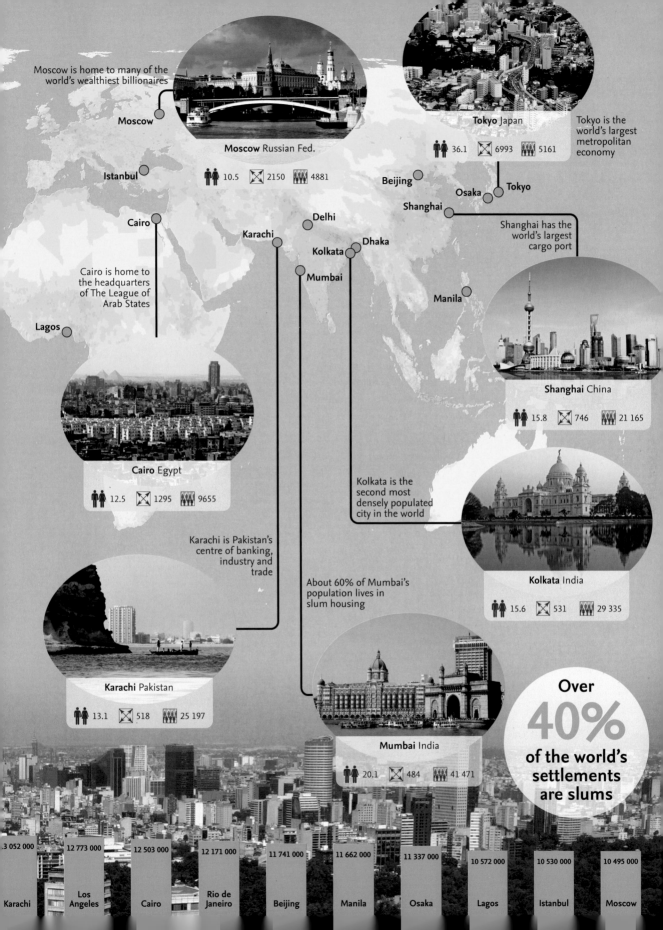

Moscow is home to many of the world's wealthiest billionaires

Moscow Russian Fed.

👫 10.5   ⊠ 2150   👪 4881

Tokyo Japan

👫 36.1   ⊠ 6993   👪 5161

Tokyo is the world's largest metropolitan economy

Istanbul

Beijing

Cairo

Karachi   Delhi

Dhaka

Kolkata

Mumbai

Osaka   Tokyo

Shanghai

Manila

Cairo is home to the headquarters of The League of Arab States

Shanghai has the world's largest cargo port

Lagos

Cairo Egypt

👫 12.5   ⊠ 1295   👪 9655

Shanghai China

👫 15.8   ⊠ 746   👪 21 165

Kolkata is the second most densely populated city in the world

Kolkata India

👫 15.6   ⊠ 531   👪 29 335

Karachi is Pakistan's centre of banking, industry and trade

About 60% of Mumbai's population lives in slum housing

Karachi Pakistan

👫 13.1   ⊠ 518   👪 25 197

Mumbai India

👫 20.1   ⊠ 484   👪 41 471

Over **40%** of the world's settlements are slums

3 052 000 | 12 773 000 | 12 503 000 | 12 171 000 | 11 741 000 | 11 662 000 | 11 337 000 | 10 572 000 | 10 530 000 | 10 495 000

Karachi | Los Angeles | Cairo | Rio de Janeiro | Beijing | Manila | Osaka | Lagos | Istanbul | Moscow

Megacities

A megacity is a metropolitan area with a total population in excess of 10 million people. In addition, some definitions set the minimum level for population density at 2000 people per square kilometre. A megacity can be a single metropolitan area or two or more metropolitan areas that converge.

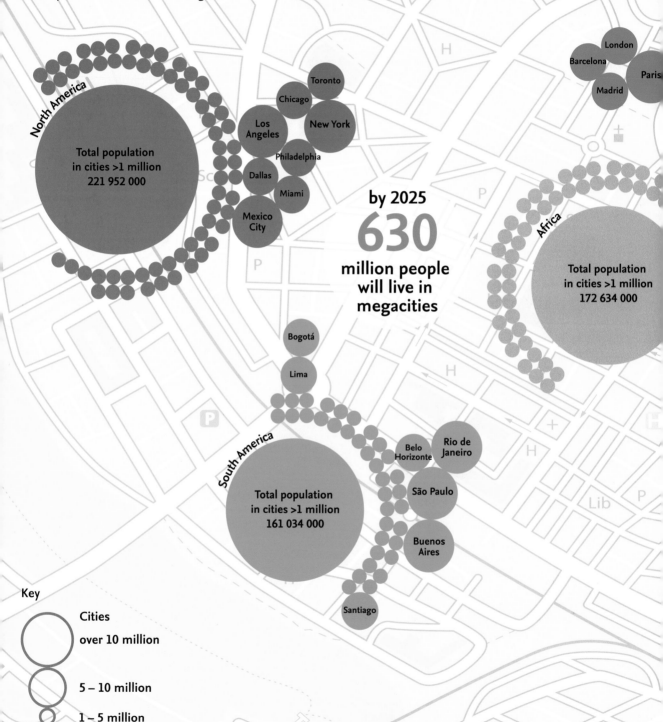

North America

Total population
in cities >1 million
221 952 000

Toronto
Chicago
Los Angeles
New York
Philadelphia
Dallas
Miami
Mexico City

London
Barcelona
Paris
Madrid

Africa

Total population
in cities >1 million
172 634 000

by 2025
630
million people
will live in
megacities

Bogotá
Lima

South America

Total population
in cities >1 million
161 034 000

Belo Horizonte
Rio de Janeiro
São Paulo
Buenos Aires
Santiago

Key

Cities

over 10 million

5 – 10 million

1 – 5 million

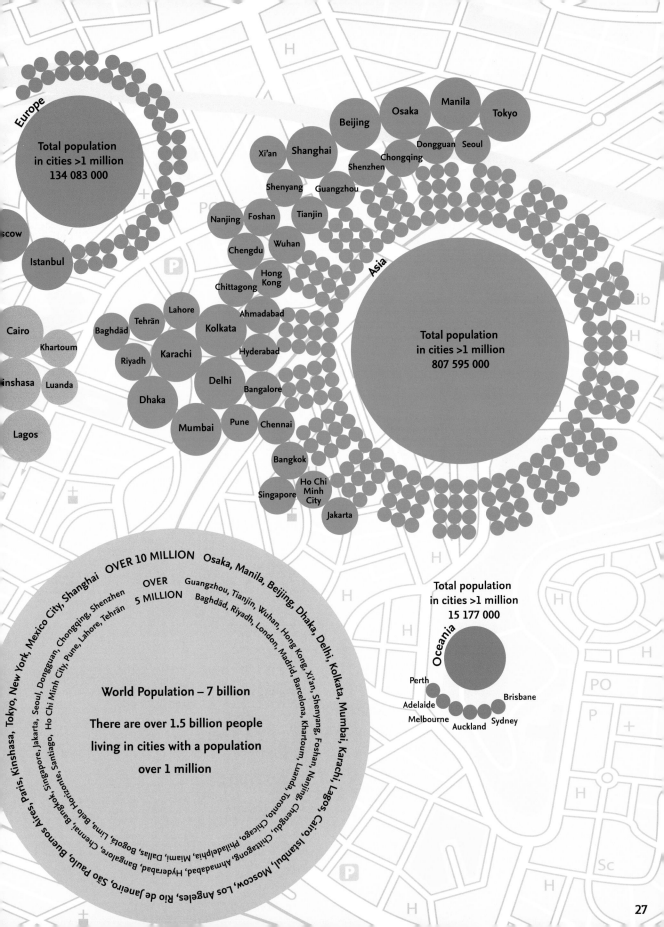

Europe

Total population
in cities >1 million
134 083 000

...scow

Istanbul

Cairo

Khartoum

...inshasa

Luanda

Lagos

Xi'an

Shanghai

Beijing

Osaka

Manila

Tokyo

Dongguan

Seoul

Chongqing

Shenzhen

Shenyang

Guangzhou

Nanjing

Foshan

Tianjin

Chengdu

Wuhan

Hong
Kong

Chittagong

Asia

Lahore

Ahmadabad

Tehrān

Baghdād

Kolkata

Riyadh

Karachi

Hyderabad

Dhaka

Delhi

Bangalore

Mumbai

Pune

Chennai

Bangkok

Ho Chi
Minh
City

Singapore

Jakarta

Total population
in cities >1 million
807 595 000

Total population
in cities >1 million
15 177 000

Oceania

Perth

Adelaide

Melbourne

Auckland

Sydney

Brisbane

OVER 10 MILLION   Osaka, Manila, Beijing, Dhaka, Delhi, Kolkata, Mumbai, Karachi, Lagos, Cairo, Istanbul, Moscow, Los Angeles, Rio de Janeiro, São Paulo, Buenos Aires, Paris, Kinshasa, Tokyo, New York, Mexico City, Shanghai

OVER 5 MILLION   Guangzhou, Tianjin, Wuhan, Hong Kong, Xi'an, Shenyang, Foshan, Nanjing, Chengdu, Chittagong, Ahmadabad, Hyderabad, Bangalore, Chennai, Bangkok, Singapore, Jakarta, Seoul, Dongguan, Chongqing, Shenzhen, Ho Chi Minh City, Pune, Lahore, Tehrān, Baghdād, Riyadh, London, Madrid, Barcelona, Khartoum, Luanda, Toronto, Chicago, Philadelphia, Miami, Dallas, Santiago, Lima, Belo Horizonte, Bogotá

World Population – 7 billion

There are over 1.5 billion people
living in cities with a population
over 1 million

Migration

The movement of people across national borders is a visible and increasingly important aspect of global integration. 3% of the world's people – more than 190 million – now live in countries in which they were not born. The forces driving the flow of migrants from poor countries to rich countries are likely to grow stronger in the future as people seek political refuge or a higher standard of living in places away from where they were born.

Annual net migration by region (million people)

Net migration is defined as the total number of immigrants less the total number of emigrants.

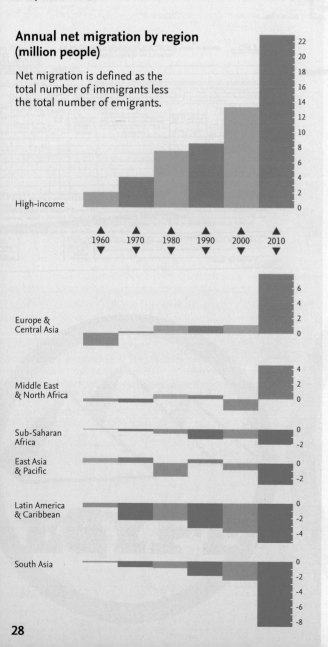

High-income

1960 1970 1980 1990 2000 2010

Europe & Central Asia

Middle East & North Africa

Sub-Saharan Africa

East Asia & Pacific

Latin America & Caribbean

South Asia

214
million
Number of International migrants worldwide

United States
42.8 million

Russian Federation
12.3 million

Germany
10.8 million

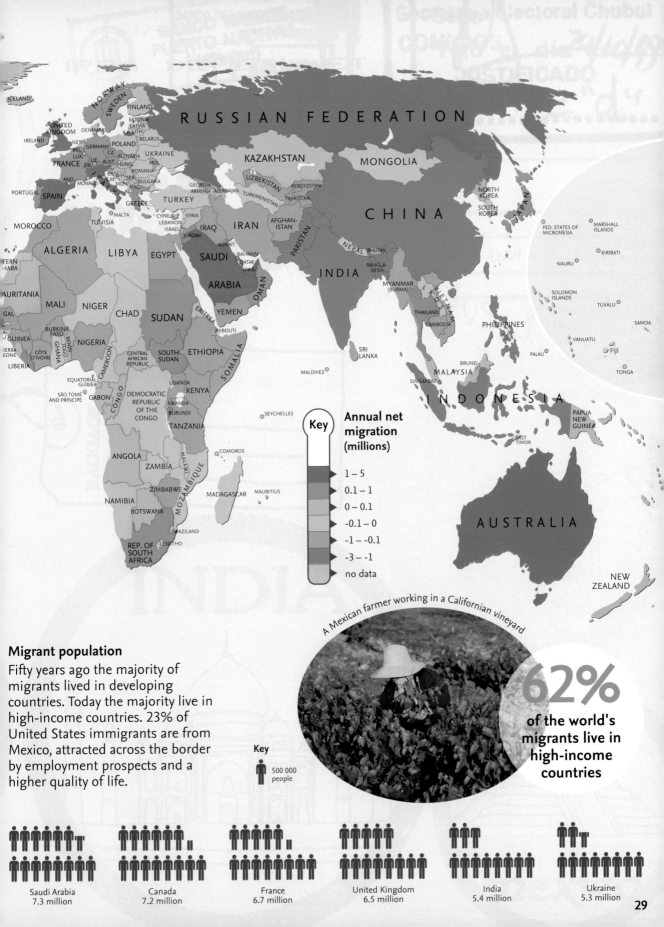

RUSSIAN FEDERATION

Annual net migration (millions)

Key

- 1 – 5
- 0.1 – 1
- 0 – 0.1
- -0.1 – 0
- -1 – -0.1
- -3 – -1
- no data

A Mexican farmer working in a Californian vineyard

62% of the world's migrants live in high-income countries

Migrant population

Fifty years ago the majority of migrants lived in developing countries. Today the majority live in high-income countries. 23% of United States immigrants are from Mexico, attracted across the border by employment prospects and a higher quality of life.

Key

👤 500 000 people

Saudi Arabia
7.3 million

Canada
7.2 million

France
6.7 million

United Kingdom
6.5 million

India
5.4 million

Ukraine
5.3 million

29

HEALTH & EDUCATION

Literacy

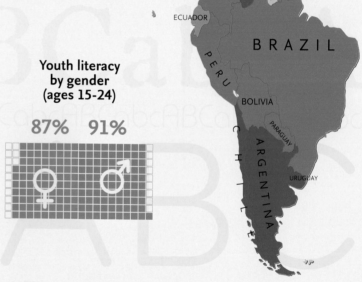

49 countries have adult literacy rates below 79%

Literacy campaigns and programmes led by UNESCO and the UN have done much to improve literacy levels and world illiteracy has halved over the last 40 years. Yet estimates indicate that between 800 and 1000 million people worldwide still cannot read or write. Illiteracy lowers a person's health and employment prospects and it makes them more expensive to train. High levels of illiteracy impede economic growth which reduces capital available for education, thus perpetuating a vicious circle of poor education and poverty.

Youth literacy by gender (ages 15-24)

87% ♀ 91% ♂

Increase in literacy

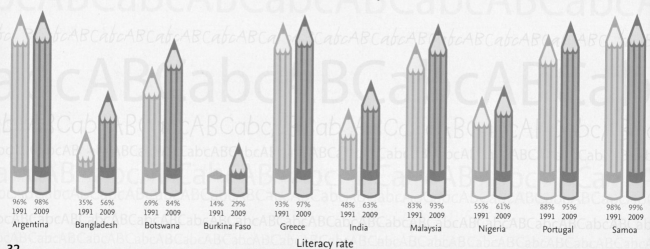

	Argentina	Bangladesh	Botswana	Burkina Faso	Greece	India	Malaysia	Nigeria	Portugal	Samoa
1991	96%	35%	69%	14%	93%	48%	83%	55%	88%	98%
2009	98%	56%	84%	29%	97%	63%	93%	61%	95%	99%

Literacy rate

Adult literacy rate

Key

	95 – 100
	89 – 94.9
	83.9 – 88.9
	60 – 83.8
	40 – 59.9
	0 – 39.9
	no data

Data excludes more developed countries. Assumes literacy rate of 95–100%

64%

of all illiterate adults are women

Adult literacy by region

Literacy rate

	95 – 100%
	83.9 – 94.9%
	0 – 83.8%
	no data

The literacy rate is defined as the percentage of the population over 15 years who can read and write.

% of population

100

80

60

40

1985   1990   1995   2000   2005   2009

High-income

Sub-Saharan Africa

South Asia

School Enrolment

Education prepares children to participate in society and to find a place in the world of work. School enrolment rates are rising, but many children still grow up without access to a basic education. There are many reasons why children do not get even a primary education. Schools may be inaccessible or of poor quality, parents may keep children at home because of high education costs or there may be demands for children's labour and their income. Ensuring that these factors are overcome and that all children receive a good quality education is the foundation of sustainable development and poverty alleviation.

Primary enrolment

GREENLAND (Denmark)

U.S.A.

C A N A D A

UNITED STATES OF AMERICA

MEXICO

THE BAHAMAS

CUBA

HAITI

DOMINICAN REP.

ST KITTS AND NEVIS

ANTIGUA AND BARBUDA

PUERTO RICO (USA)

DOMINICA

ST LUCIA

ST VINCENT AND THE GRENADINES

BARBADOS

GRENADA

TRINIDAD & TOBAGO

BELIZE

JAMAICA

GUATEMALA

HONDURAS

EL SALVADOR

NICARAGUA

COSTA RICA

PANAMA

VENEZUELA

GUYANA

SURINAME

FRENCH GUIANA

COLOMBIA

ECUADOR

CAPE

B R A Z I L

P E R U

BOLIVIA

PARAGUAY

C H I L E

ARGENTINA

URUGUAY

67% of children complete primary school in Sub-Saharan Africa

Key

Primary school enrolment (% net)

- 95 – 100
- 90 – 94.9
- 86.9 – 89.9
- 80 – 86.8
- 70 – 79.9
- 35 – 69.9
- no data

Secondary enrolment

In Chad, only **29%** of secondary school pupils are female

Secondary school enrolment (% net)

- 85 – 100
- 75 – 84.9
- 58.8 – 74.9
- 40 – 58.7
- 25 – 39.9
- 0 – 24.9
- no data

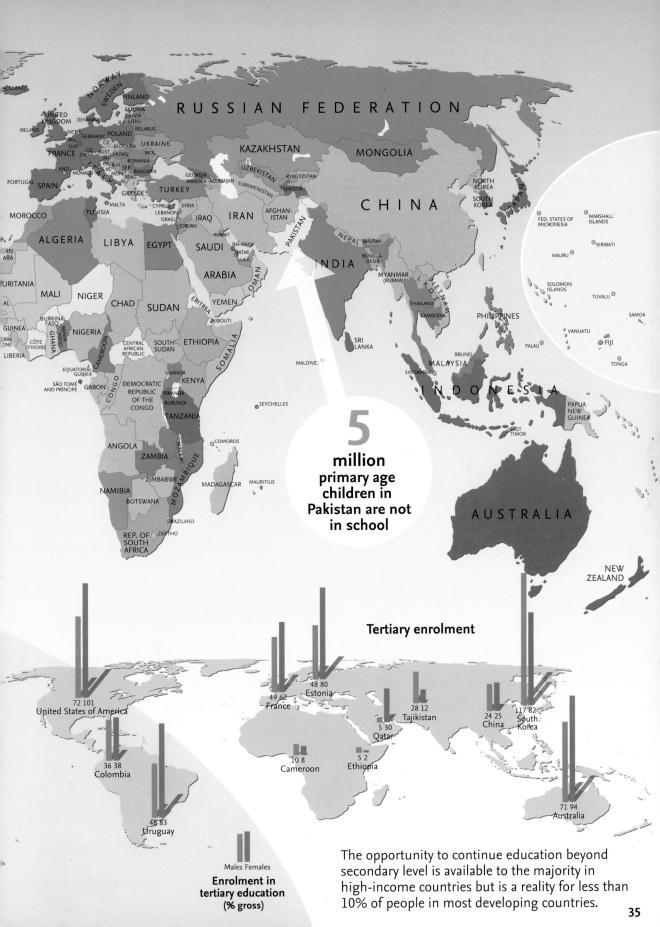

5 million primary age children in Pakistan are not in school

Tertiary enrolment

72 101
United States of America

49 62
France

48 80
Estonia

28 12
Tajikistan

5 30
Qatar

24 25
China

117 82
South Korea

36 38
Colombia

10 8
Cameroon

5 2
Ethiopia

71 94
Australia

48 83
Uruguay

Males Females

Enrolment in tertiary education (% gross)

The opportunity to continue education beyond secondary level is available to the majority in high-income countries but is a reality for less than 10% of people in most developing countries.

35

Birth and Fertility Rates

A fertility rate of two children per woman is considered the replacement rate with levels lower than this indicating a declining population – assuming this is not outweighed by migration. Levels much higher than this indicate a growing population. Because of high mortality and fertility rates women in Africa face a 1 in 22 risk of a pregnancy related death compared to a risk of only 1 in 6700 to women in high-income countries.

Births attended by skilled health staff

99%
High-income economies

65%
World

45%
Sub-Saharan Africa

Maternal mortality

Inadequate healthcare before, during and after pregnancy results in high maternal mortality rates in many countries.

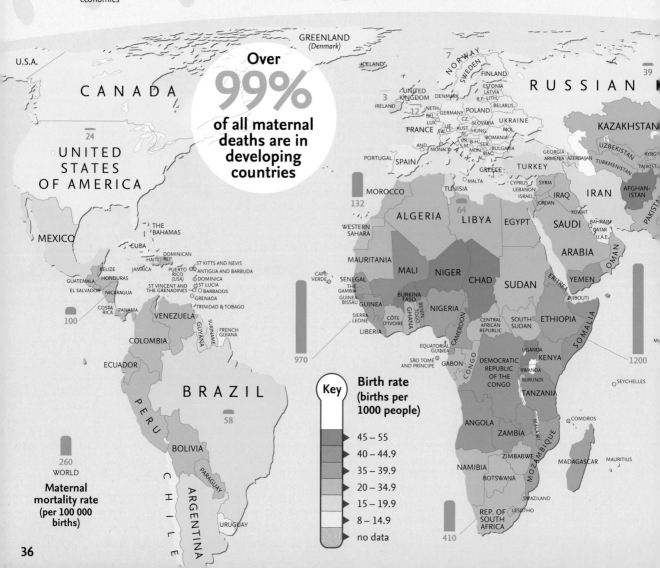

Over **99%** of all maternal deaths are in developing countries

Key

Birth rate (births per 1000 people)

- 45 – 55
- 40 – 44.9
- 35 – 39.9
- 20 – 34.9
- 15 – 19.9
- 8 – 14.9
- no data

Maternal mortality rate (per 100 000 births)

132 — MOROCCO
64 — (Tunisia)
100 — (Central America)
970 —
1200 —
58 — BRAZIL
260 WORLD
410 — REP. OF SOUTH AFRICA
24 — (USA)
7 — NORWAY
3 — IRELAND
12 —
39 —

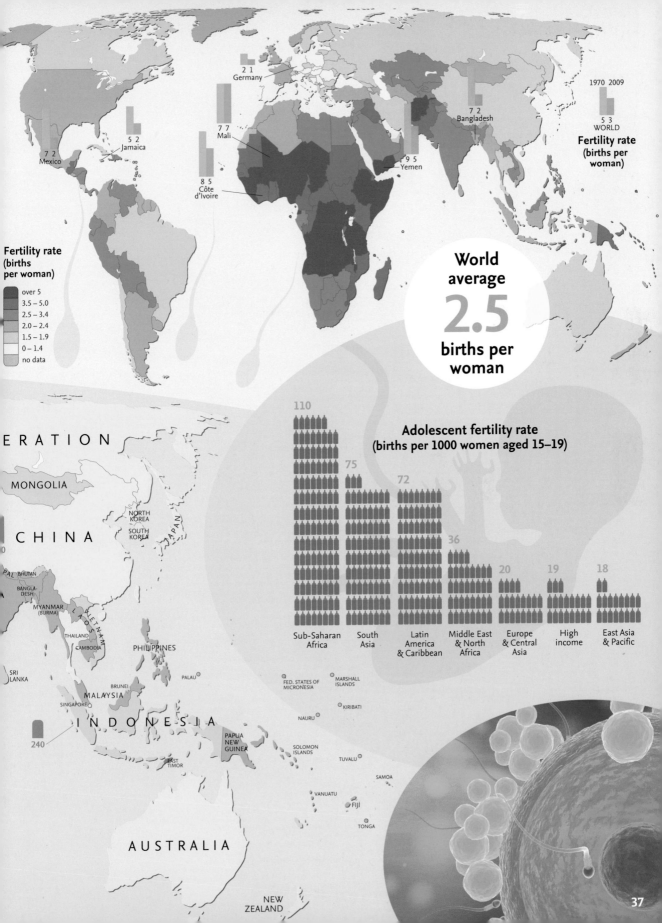

Fertility rate
(births per woman)

over 5
3.5 – 5.0
2.5 – 3.4
2.0 – 2.4
1.5 – 1.9
0 – 1.4
no data

2 1
Germany

7 7
Mali

5 2
Jamaica

7 2
Mexico

8 5
Côte d'Ivoire

9 5
Yemen

7 2
Bangladesh

1970 2009
5 3
WORLD

Fertility rate
(births per woman)

World average
2.5
births per woman

Adolescent fertility rate
(births per 1000 women aged 15–19)

110 — Sub-Saharan Africa
75 — South Asia
72 — Latin America & Caribbean
36 — Middle East & North Africa
20 — Europe & Central Asia
19 — High income
18 — East Asia & Pacific

ERATION

MONGOLIA

CHINA

NORTH KOREA

SOUTH KOREA

JAPAN

NEPAL BHUTAN

BANGLA-DESH

MYANMAR (BURMA)

LAOS

VIETNAM

THAILAND

CAMBODIA

PHILIPPINES

SRI LANKA

BRUNEI

MALAYSIA

SINGAPORE

INDONESIA

240

EAST TIMOR

PALAU

PAPUA NEW GUINEA

FED. STATES OF MICRONESIA

MARSHALL ISLANDS

NAURU

KIRIBATI

SOLOMON ISLANDS

TUVALU

SAMOA

VANUATU

FIJI

TONGA

AUSTRALIA

NEW ZEALAND

Maternal Health

Arab World	East Asia & Pacific	Europe & Central Asia	Latin America & Caribbean
41.9	18	20.4	72.3
26.2	13.7	12.6	18.8
71.7	89.2	–	89.5
46.7	76	–	74.7
3.3	1.8	1.7	2.3
171	1060	456	295

$244

$407

$2174

$545

Only **19%** of total births in South Sudan are attended by skilled health staff

 Adolescent fertility rate (births per 1,000 women ages 15-19)

 Births attended by skilled health staff

 Fertility rate (births per woman)

Crude birth rate (per 1000 people)

 Contraceptive prevalence (% of women ages 15-49)

 Female population (millions)

Chronic hunger occurs when the short fall of dietary energy exceeds

300 Kilocalories

FEDERATION

KAZAKHSTAN

AN

UZBEKISTAN
TURKMENISTAN
KYRGYZSTAN
TAJIKISTAN

MONGOLIA

IRAN

AFGHAN-
ISTAN

PAKISTAN

CHINA

NORTH
KOREA

SOUTH
KOREA

JAPAN

BAHRAIN
QATAR
U.A.E.
OI

OMAN

INDIA

NEPAL
BHUTAN

BANGLA-
DESH

MYANMAR
(BURMA)

LAOS

VIETNAM

THAILAND

CAMBODIA

PHILIPPINES

SRI
LANKA

MALDIVES

SINGAPORE

MALAYSIA

BRUNEI

INDONESIA

PALAU

FED. STATES OF
MICRONESIA

MARSHALL
ISLANDS

KIRIBATI

NAURU

Lack of vitamin A kills a million infants a year

PAPUA
NEW
GUINEA

SOLOMON
ISLANDS

TUVALU

EAST
TIMOR

SAMOA

VANUATU

FIJI

TONGA

SEYCHELLES

OROS

GASCAR

MAURITIUS

104 million children are under nourished

AUSTRALIA

NEW
ZEALAND

A child dies every 6 seconds from hunger-related causes

Daily caloric intake

Key = 250 kcal per capita

Recommended daily intake for a male = 2500 kcal

China
2940

Dem. Rep. of the Congo
1606

India
2473

Sweden
3208

United States of America
3754

47

Immunization

The graphic below illustrate the growth in immunization programmes, for selected diseases, between 1999 and 2008.

Tuberculosis

95%
East Asia & Pacific
88%

84%
Least developed countries
74%

Sub-Saharan Africa
65%
81%

84%
96%
Latin America & Caribbean
92%

Middle East & North Africa
92%

89%
World
81%

89%
Developing countries
80%

88%
South Asia
74%

an estimated
19.3
million infants worldwide are not reached by routine immunization services.

Polio

94%
East Asia & Pacific
87%

Least developed countries
59%
77%

Sub-Saharan Africa
50%
71%

92%
Latin America & Caribbean
91%

91
Middle East & North Africa
89%

83%
World
76%

81%
Developing countries
74%

87%
South Asia
73%

Life threatening infectious diseases can be averted by the administration of vaccines to stimulate the body's own immune system and protect against further infection. It is one of the most cost effective health investments and can prevent between two and three million deaths each year.

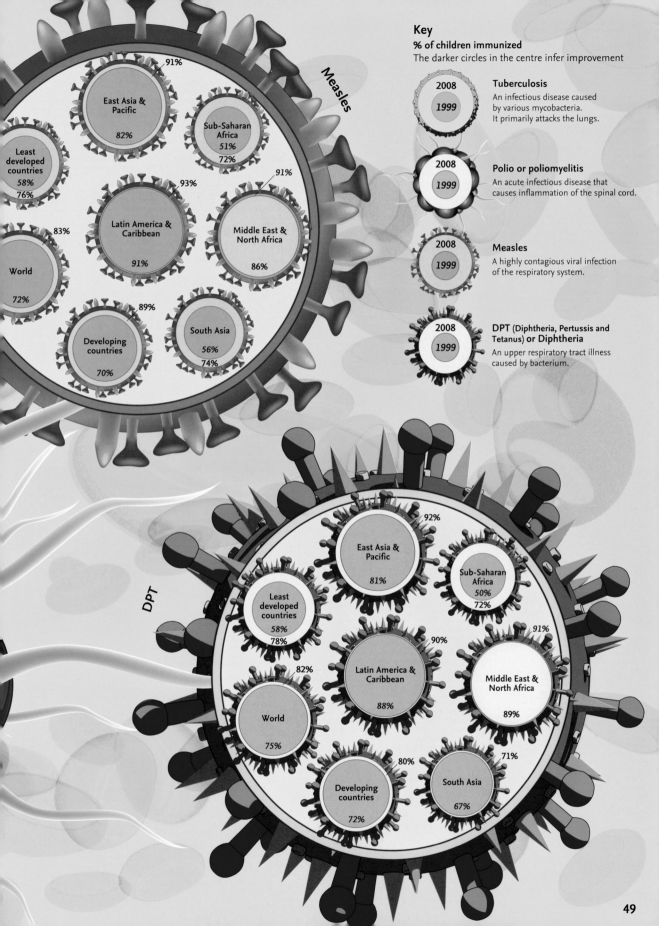

Measles

East Asia & Pacific
82%
91%

Sub-Saharan Africa
51%
72%

Least developed countries
58%
76%

Latin America & Caribbean
91%
93%

Middle East & North Africa
86%
91%

World
72%
83%

Developing countries
70%
89%

South Asia
56%
74%

Key
% of children immunized
The darker circles in the centre infer improvement

2008
1999

Tuberculosis
An infectious disease caused by various mycobacteria. It primarily attacks the lungs.

2008
1999

Polio or poliomyelitis
An acute infectious disease that causes inflammation of the spinal cord.

2008
1999

Measles
A highly contagious viral infection of the respiratory system.

2008
1999

DPT (Diphtheria, Pertussis and Tetanus) **or Diphtheria**
An upper respiratory tract illness caused by bacterium.

DPT

East Asia & Pacific
81%
92%

Sub-Saharan Africa
50%
72%

Least developed countries
58%
78%

Latin America & Caribbean
88%
90%

Middle East & North Africa
89%
91%

World
75%
82%

Developing countries
72%
80%

South Asia
67%
71%

Health Provision

Communicable diseases such as HIV/AIDS, tuberculosis and malaria kill millions of people each year. They exact a terrible toll on society and the economy of developing countries. Although international awareness and funding to fight epidemic diseases have increased, much remains to be done. Immunization is a proven way of combating life-threatening infectious disease and it is estimated that it prevents over 2 million deaths a year.

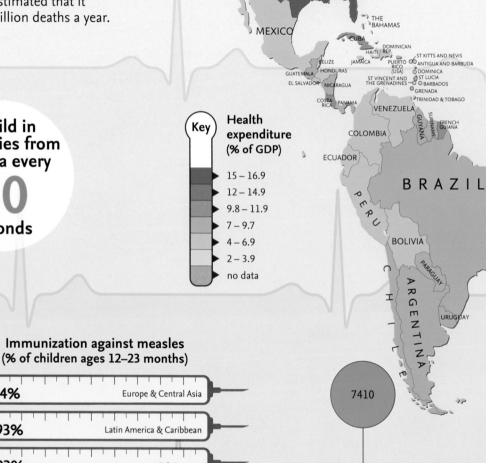

A child in Africa dies from malaria every

30

seconds

Key — Health expenditure (% of GDP)

- 15 – 16.9
- 12 – 14.9
- 9.8 – 11.9
- 7 – 9.7
- 4 – 6.9
- 2 – 3.9
- no data

Immunization against measles
(% of children ages 12–23 months)

- **94%** Europe & Central Asia
- **93%** Latin America & Caribbean
- **93%** High-income
- **91%** East Asia & Pacific
- **87%** Middle East & North Africa
- **74%** South Asia
- **68%** Sub-Saharan Africa

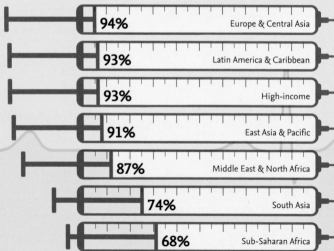

7410

734

201

2

U.S.A. Peru Brazil Mauritania

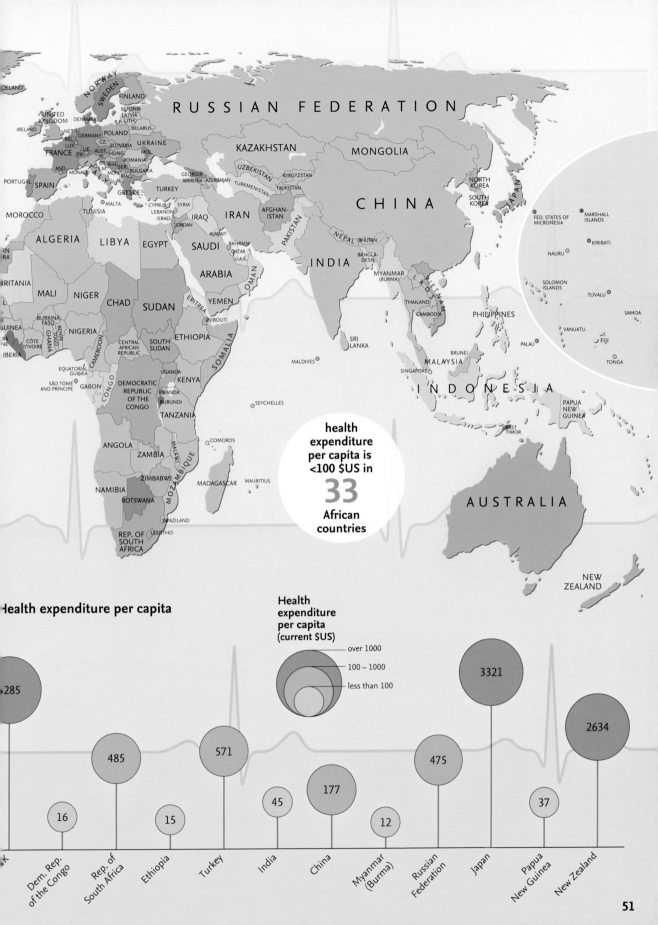

ICELAND
NORWAY
SWEDEN
FINLAND
UNITED
KINGDOM
IRELAND
DENMARK
ESTONIA
LATVIA
R.F. LITH.
BELARUS
NETH.
BEL.
GERMANY
POLAND
UKRAINE
FRANCE
LUX.
CZ.
SLOVAKIA
MOLD.
AUST.
HUNG.
ROMANIA
AND.
SW.
LIE.
SLO.
CR.
B-H.
SER.
BULGARIA
MONACO
ITALY
MON.
MAC.
AL.
PORTUGAL
SPAIN
GREECE
TURKEY
MALTA
CYPRUS
SYRIA
LEBANON
ISRAEL
JORDAN
GEORGIA
ARMENIA
AZERBAIJAN
TURKMENISTAN
TAJIKISTAN

RUSSIAN FEDERATION

KAZAKHSTAN
MONGOLIA
UZBEKISTAN
KYRGYZSTAN

CHINA

NORTH
KOREA
SOUTH
KOREA
JAPAN

FED. STATES OF
MICRONESIA
MARSHALL
ISLANDS
KIRIBATI
NAURU

MOROCCO
ALGERIA
LIBYA
EGYPT
TUNISIA
MAURITANIA
MALI
NIGER
CHAD
SUDAN
SAUDI
ARABIA
IRAN
IRAQ
KUWAIT
BAHRAIN
QATAR
U.A.E.
OMAN
YEMEN
AFGHAN-
ISTAN
PAKISTAN
NEPAL
BHUTAN
BANGLA-
DESH
INDIA
MYANMAR
(BURMA)
ERITREA
DJIBOUTI

SENEGAL
GUINEA
BURKINA
FASO
BENIN
TOGO
GHANA
NIGERIA
CÔTE
D'IVOIRE
LIBERIA
CAMEROON
CENTRAL
AFRICAN
REPUBLIC
SOUTH
SUDAN
ETHIOPIA
SOMALIA
EQUATORIAL
GUINEA
GABON
SÃO TOMÉ
AND PRÍNCIPE
CONGO
DEMOCRATIC
REPUBLIC
OF THE
CONGO
UGANDA
KENYA
RWANDA
BURUNDI
TANZANIA
MALDIVES
SRI
LANKA
SEYCHELLES
THAILAND
LAOS
VIETNAM
CAMBODIA
PHILIPPINES
BRUNEI
MALAYSIA
SINGAPORE

INDONESIA
PALAU
SOLOMON
ISLANDS
TUVALU
VANUATU
FIJI
SAMOA
TONGA

ANGOLA
ZAMBIA
MALAWI
MOZAMBIQUE
COMOROS
MADAGASCAR
MAURITIUS
ZIMBABWE
NAMIBIA
BOTSWANA
SWAZILAND
LESOTHO
REP. OF
SOUTH
AFRICA

EAST
TIMOR
PAPUA
NEW
GUINEA

AUSTRALIA

NEW
ZEALAND

**health
expenditure
per capita is
<100 $US in**

33

**African
countries**

Health expenditure per capita

**Health
expenditure
per capita
(current $US)**

over 1000
100 – 1000
less than 100

285

485

571

45

177

12

475

3321

37

2634

16

15

...k

Dem. Rep.
of the Congo

Rep. of
South Africa

Ethiopia

Turkey

India

China

Myanmar
(Burma)

Russian
Federation

Japan

Papua
New Guinea

New Zealand

HIV/AIDS

AIDS stands for Acquired Immune Deficiency Syndrome. It is caused by the Human Immunodeficiency Virus (HIV), which reduces the life expectancy and diminishes the quality of life of the average citizen. Levels of infection are highest in Sub-Saharan Africa where the spread of the virus has been relentless over the last 25 years.

Top 10 countries with highest prevalence of HIV

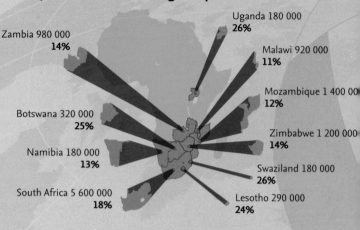

Uganda 180 000
26%

Zambia 980 000
14%

Malawi 920 000
11%

Mozambique 1 400 000
12%

Botswana 320 000
25%

Zimbabwe 1 200 000
14%

Namibia 180 000
13%

Swaziland 180 000
26%

South Africa 5 600 000
18%

Lesotho 290 000
24%

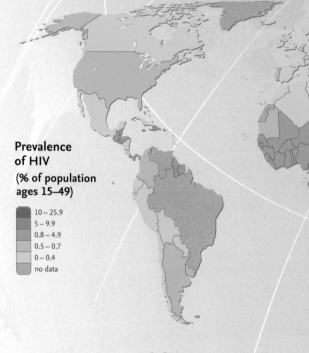

Prevalence of HIV

(% of population ages 15–49)

- 10 – 25.9
- 5 – 9.9
- 0.8 – 4.9
- 0.5 – 0.7
- 0 – 0.4
- no data

5500
people die from AIDS every day

Human immunodeficiency virus (HIV)

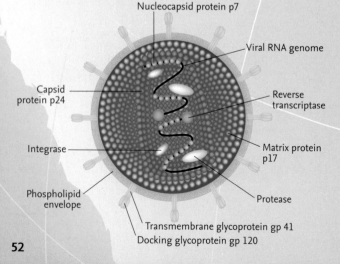

Nucleocapsid protein p7

Viral RNA genome

Capsid protein p24

Reverse transcriptase

Integrase

Matrix protein p17

Phospholipid envelope

Protease

Transmembrane glycoprotein gp 41

Docking glycoprotein gp 120

Impact of HIV/AIDS on life expectancy in Southern Africa

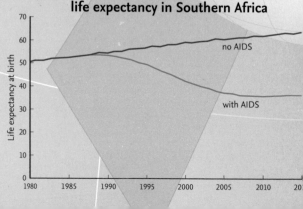

no AIDS

with AIDS

Life expectancy at birth

70 / 60 / 50 / 40 / 30 / 20 / 10 / 0

1980 / 1985 / 1990 / 1995 / 2000 / 2005 / 2010 / 20

What is HIV?

HIV is a lentivirus that attacks the immune system

How does it work?

HIV destroys T-cells, a type of blood cell that protects the body from infection

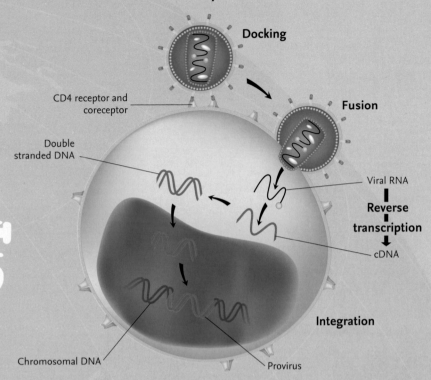

HIV Entry to T Cell

Docking

CD4 receptor and coreceptor

Double stranded DNA

Fusion

Viral RNA

Reverse transcription

cDNA

Chromosomal DNA

Provirus

Integration

How can you get it?

Male-to-male sexual contact **61%**

Infection from drug use **19%**

High risk heterosexual contact **11%**

Others **1%**

Male to male sexual contact and Infection drug use **8%**

What are the symptoms?

A person can be infected with the HIV virus for years before it is detected. Eventually the virus begins to destroy immune cells leaving the body incapable of fighting off infection.

Current State of HIV/AIDS

AMERICA

1.1 million Americans are estimated to have HIV

About 55 000 new infections occur each year in the US

GLOBAL

60 million have been infected and 30 million have died of AIDS

AFRICA

67% are living with HIV/AIDS

91% of new infections are among children

72% of deaths from AIDS worldwide occur in Africa

Medical Care

In some nations concern about the length of hospital waiting lists reaches the news headlines whilst in other countries medical staff are still struggling to provide even the most basic health care service. High-income countries tend to have more doctors per person than low- or middle-income economies but there are exceptions – many countries of the former Soviet Union have very high rates of access. Healthcare facilities and quality of treatment can vary greatly both between and within countries. The availability of a hospital bed may mean anything from a private room in a well equipped hospital to an overcrowded bed in a rural clinic many hours walk away. Likewise a doctor may mean anything from a highly qualified specialist surgeon to a recently trained medical assistant.

Hospital beds

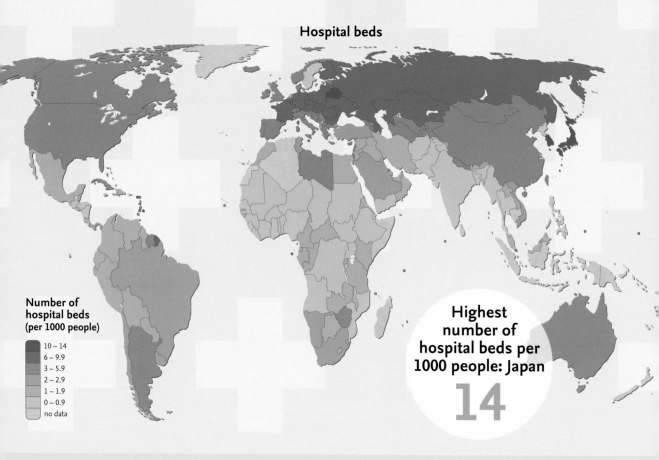

Number of hospital beds (per 1000 people)

- 10 – 14
- 6 – 9.9
- 3 – 5.9
- 2 – 2.9
- 1 – 1.9
- 0 – 0.9
- no data

Highest number of hospital beds per 1000 people: Japan

14

Health indicators

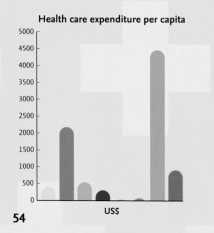

Health care expenditure per capita

US$

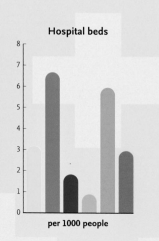

Hospital beds

per 1000 people

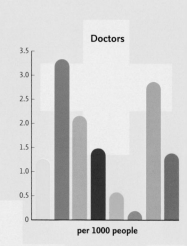

Doctors

per 1000 people

54

Number of doctors

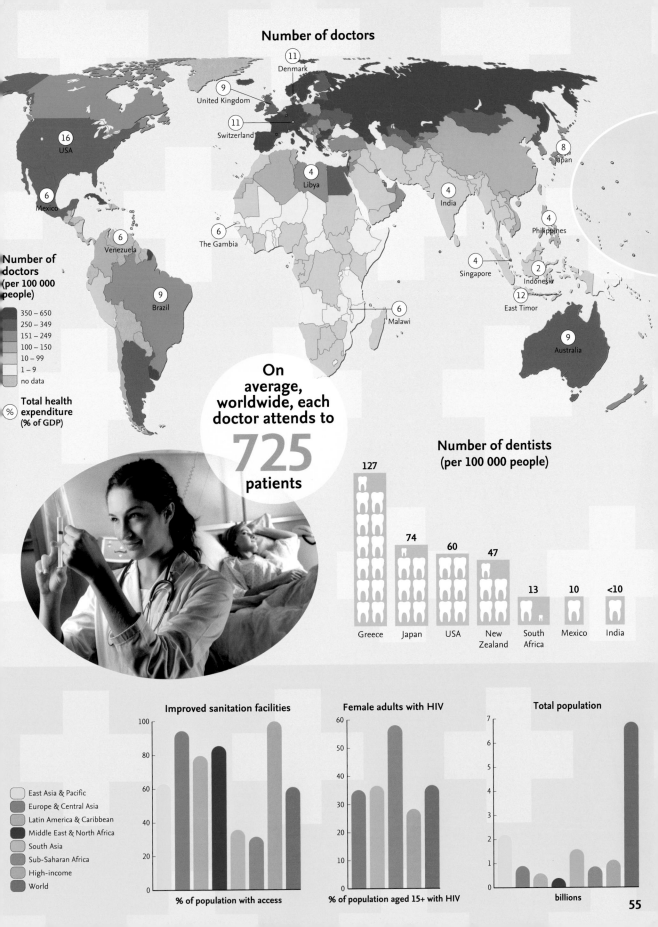

(11) Denmark

(9) United Kingdom

(11) Switzerland

(16) USA

(6) Mexico

(6) Venezuela

(9) Brazil

(4) Libya

(6) The Gambia

(6) Malawi

(4) India

(8) Japan

(4) Philippines

(4) Singapore

(2) Indonesia

(12) East Timor

(9) Australia

Number of doctors (per 100 000 people)

- 350 – 650
- 250 – 349
- 151 – 249
- 100 – 150
- 10 – 99
- 1 – 9
- no data

% Total health expenditure (% of GDP)

On average, worldwide, each doctor attends to

725

patients

Number of dentists (per 100 000 people)

127	74	60	47	13	10	<10
Greece	Japan	USA	New Zealand	South Africa	Mexico	India

Improved sanitation facilities

100
80
60
40
20
0

% of population with access

Female adults with HIV

60
50
40
30
20
10
0

% of population aged 15+ with HIV

Total population

7
6
5
4
3
2
1
0

billions

Legend:
- East Asia & Pacific
- Europe & Central Asia
- Latin America & Caribbean
- Middle East & North Africa
- South Asia
- Sub-Saharan Africa
- High-income
- World

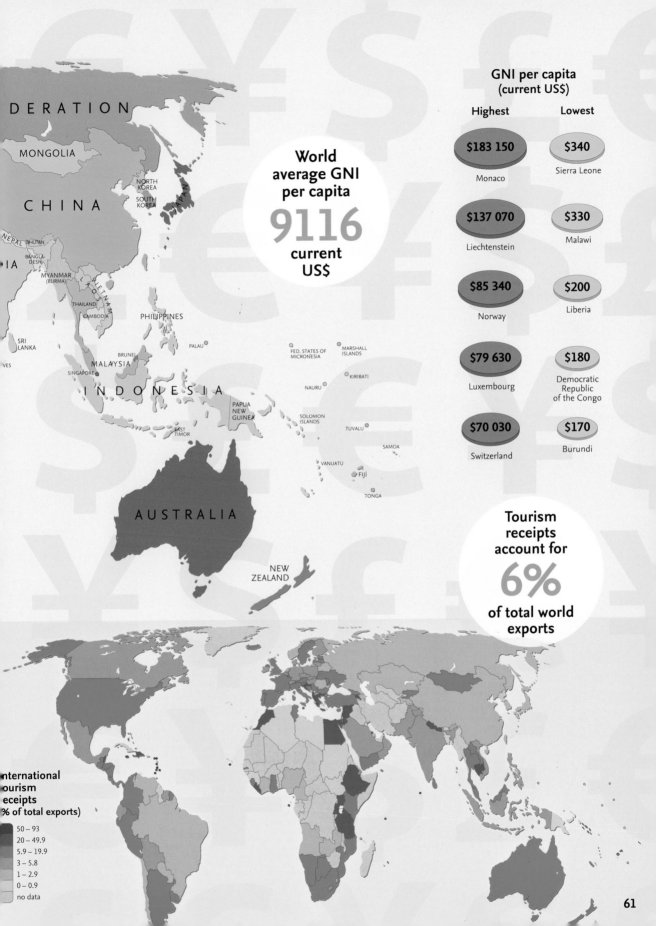

MONGOLIA

DERATION

NORTH KOREA

SOUTH KOREA

JAPAN

CHINA

NEPAL BHUTAN

BANGLA-DESH

MYANMAR (BURMA)

LAOS

VIETNAM

THAILAND

CAMBODIA

PHILIPPINES

SRI LANKA

VES

MALAYSIA

BRUNEI

SINGAPORE

INDONESIA

IA

PALAU

FED. STATES OF MICRONESIA

MARSHALL ISLANDS

NAURU

KIRIBATI

PAPUA NEW GUINEA

SOLOMON ISLANDS

TUVALU

EAST TIMOR

SAMOA

VANUATU

FIJI

TONGA

AUSTRALIA

NEW ZEALAND

World average GNI per capita
9116
current US$

GNI per capita
(current US$)

Highest	Lowest
$183 150	**$340**
Monaco	Sierra Leone
$137 070	**$330**
Liechtenstein	Malawi
$85 340	**$200**
Norway	Liberia
$79 630	**$180**
Luxembourg	Democratic Republic of the Congo
$70 030	**$170**
Switzerland	Burundi

Tourism receipts account for
6%
of total world exports

International Tourism Receipts
(% of total exports)

50 – 93
20 – 49.9
5.9 – 19.9
3 – 5.8
1 – 2.9
0 – 0.9
no data

61

Most Visited Countries

Tourism is a popular global leisure activity and is an important industry for many countries. It brings in large amounts of income for goods and services available and contributes an estimated 5% to the worldwide Gross Domestic Product. It also creates opportunities for employment in the service industries associated with tourism.

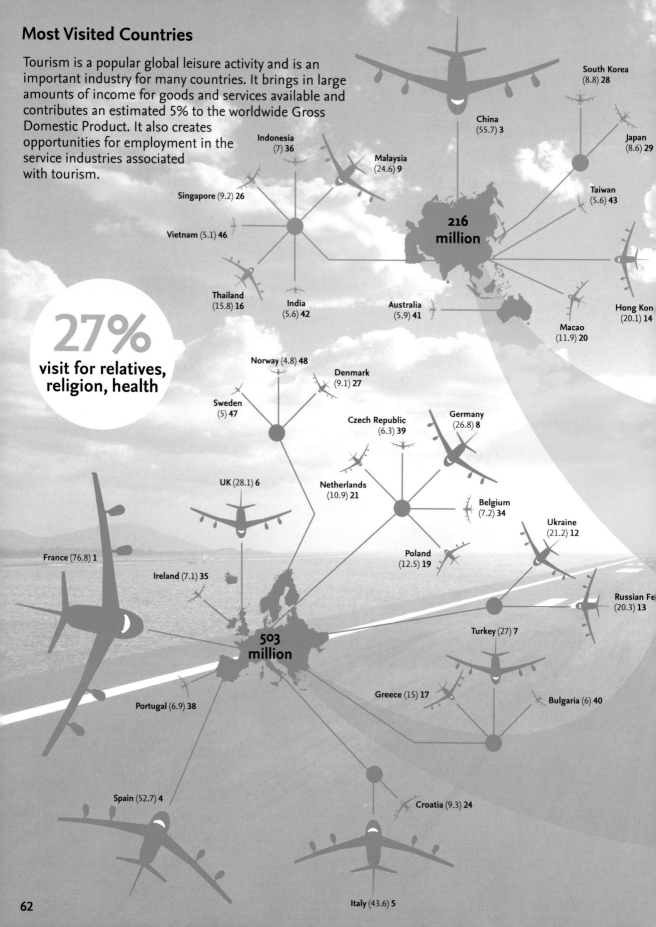

27%
visit for relatives, religion, health

216 million

South Korea (8.8) 28
China (55.7) 3
Japan (8.6) 29
Indonesia (7) 36
Malaysia (24.6) 9
Taiwan (5.6) 43
Singapore (9.2) 26
Vietnam (5.1) 46
Thailand (15.8) 16
India (5.6) 42
Australia (5.9) 41
Hong Kon (20.1) 14
Macao (11.9) 20

503 million

Norway (4.8) 48
Denmark (9.1) 27
Sweden (5) 47
Czech Republic (6.3) 39
Germany (26.8) 8
UK (28.1) 6
Netherlands (10.9) 21
Belgium (7.2) 34
Ukraine (21.2) 12
France (76.8) 1
Ireland (7.1) 35
Poland (12.5) 19
Russian Fe (20.3) 13
Turkey (27) 7
Portugal (6.9) 38
Greece (15) 17
Bulgaria (6) 40
Spain (52.7) 4
Croatia (9.3) 24
Italy (43.6) 5

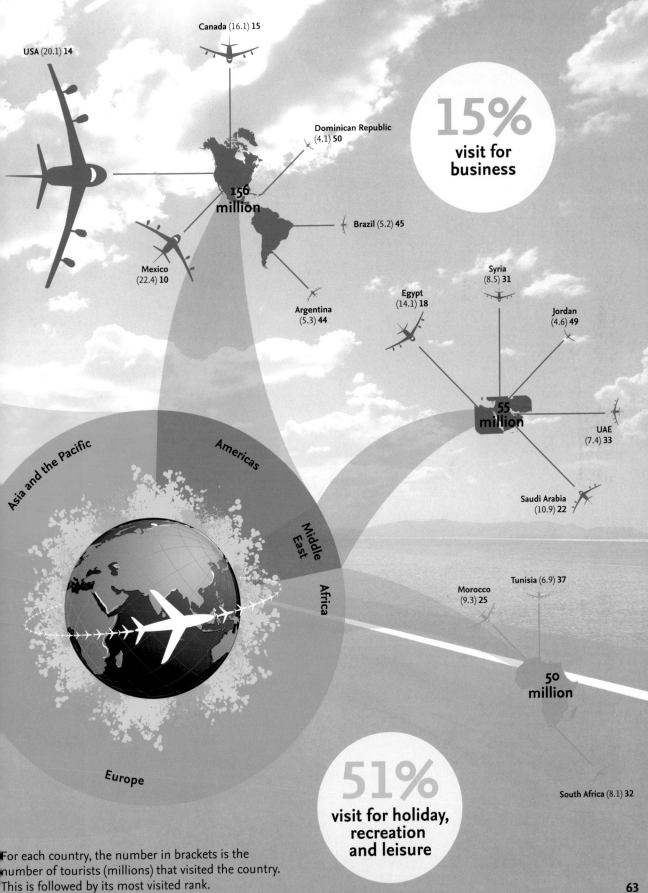

USA (20.1) **14**

Canada (16.1) **15**

Dominican Republic (4.1) **50**

15%
visit for business

156 million

Brazil (5.2) **45**

Mexico (22.4) **10**

Argentina (5.3) **44**

Syria (8.5) **31**

Egypt (14.1) **18**

Jordan (4.6) **49**

55 million

UAE (7.4) **33**

Saudi Arabia (10.9) **22**

Asia and the Pacific

Americas

Middle East

Africa

Tunisia (6.9) **37**

Morocco (9.3) **25**

50 million

Europe

51%
visit for holiday, recreation and leisure

South Africa (8.1) **32**

For each country, the number in brackets is the number of tourists (millions) that visited the country. This is followed by its most visited rank.

63

Economic Growth

Despite fluctuating markets and periods of global economic slowdown the general trend is for world economic growth. Technological improvements, increasing productivity and expanding trade all contribute to growth. Furthermore, faster growth in developing countries is reducing poverty rates and slowly closing the income gap with high-income countries. But growth must be sustained over the long term and the gains from economic growth must be shared to make lasting improvements to the well-being of all people.

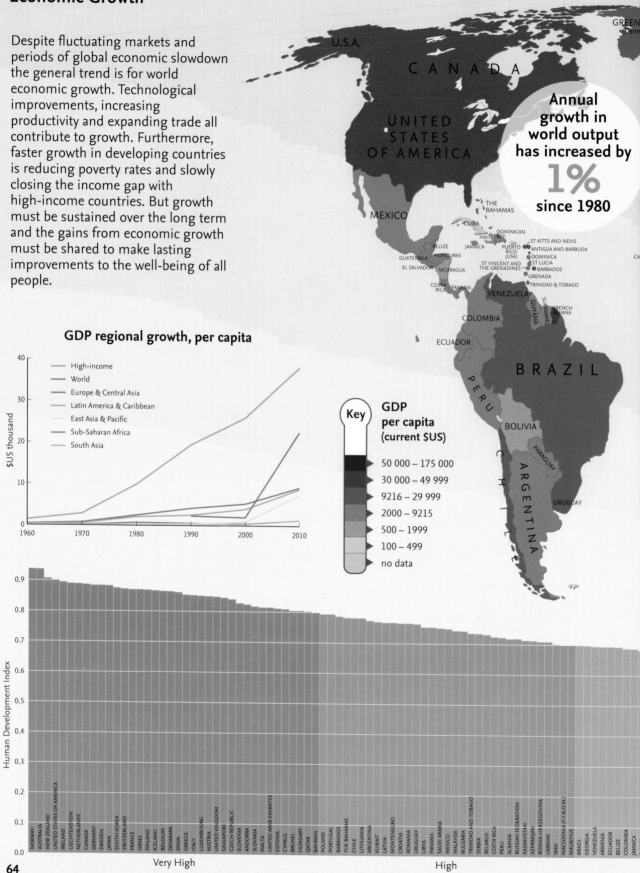

Annual growth in world output has increased by **1%** since 1980

GDP regional growth, per capita

$US thousand

- High-income
- World
- Europe & Central Asia
- Latin America & Caribbean
- East Asia & Pacific
- Sub-Saharan Africa
- South Asia

1960 1970 1980 1990 2000 2010

Key GDP per capita (current $US)

- 50 000 – 175 000
- 30 000 – 49 999
- 9216 – 29 999
- 2000 – 9215
- 500 – 1999
- 100 – 499
- no data

Human Development Index

NORWAY, AUSTRALIA, NEW ZEALAND, UNITED STATES OF AMERICA, IRELAND, LIECHTENSTEIN, NETHERLANDS, CANADA, GERMANY, SWEDEN, JAPAN, SOUTH KOREA, SWITZERLAND, FRANCE, ISRAEL, FINLAND, ICELAND, BELGIUM, DENMARK, SPAIN, GREECE, ITALY, LUXEMBOURG, AUSTRIA, UNITED KINGDOM, SINGAPORE, CZECH REPUBLIC, SLOVENIA, ANDORRA, SLOVAKIA, MALTA, UNITED ARAB EMIRATES, ESTONIA, CYPRUS, BRUNEI, HUNGARY, QATAR, BAHRAIN, POLAND, PORTUGAL, BARBADOS, THE BAHAMAS, CHILE, LITHUANIA, ARGENTINA, KUWAIT, LATVIA, MONTENEGRO, CROATIA, ROMANIA, URUGUAY, LIBYA, PANAMA, SAUDI ARABIA, MEXICO, MALAYSIA, BULGARIA, TRINIDAD AND TOBAGO, SERBIA, BELARUS, COSTA RICA, PERU, ALBANIA, RUSSIAN FEDERATION, KAZAKHSTAN, AZERBAIJAN, BOSNIA-HERZEGOVINA, UKRAINE, IRAN, MACEDONIA (F.Y.R.O.M.), MAURITIUS, GEORGIA, VENEZUELA, ARMENIA, ECUADOR, BELIZE, COLOMBIA, ...

Very High   High

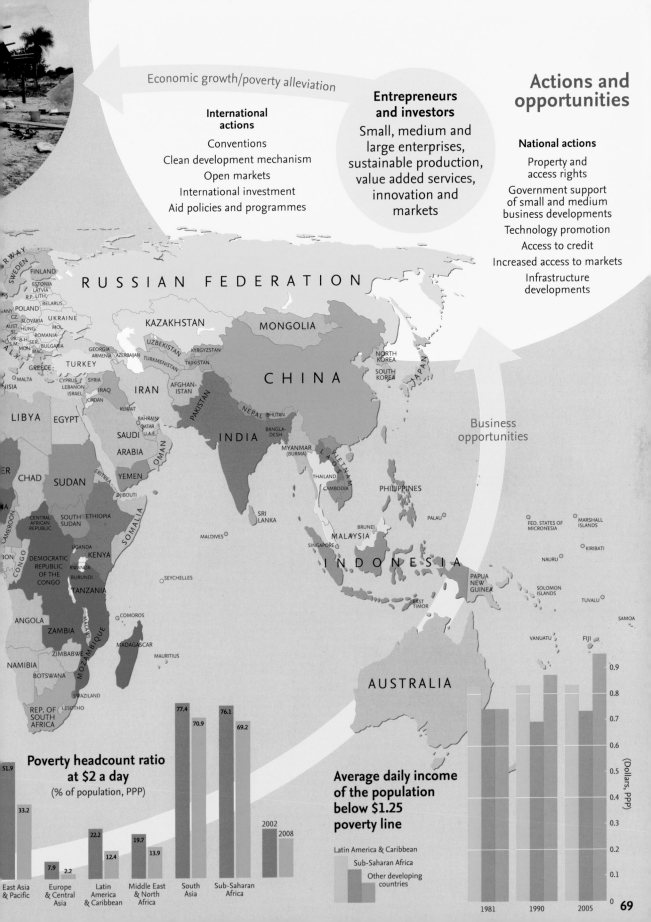

Actions and opportunities

Economic growth/poverty alleviation

International actions

Conventions
Clean development mechanism
Open markets
International investment
Aid policies and programmes

Entrepreneurs and investors

Small, medium and large enterprises, sustainable production, value added services, innovation and markets

National actions

Property and access rights
Government support of small and medium business developments
Technology promotion
Access to credit
Increased access to markets
Infrastructure developments

Business opportunities

Map labels:

R W A Y, SWEDEN, FINLAND, ESTONIA, LATVIA, R.F. LITH., BELARUS, POLAND, ANY, CZ, SLOVAKIA, UKRAINE, AUST. HUNG., MOL, SL, B-H, ROMANIA, S.M., SER, BULGARIA, MON, MAC., GREECE, TURKEY, ITALY, MALTA, CYPRUS, LEBANON, SYRIA, ISRAEL, JORDAN, IRAQ, TUNISIA, LIBYA, EGYPT, SAUDI ARABIA, YEMEN, ERITREA, DJIBOUTI, CHAD, SUDAN, SOUTH SUDAN, ETHIOPIA, SOMALIA, CENTRAL AFRICAN REPUBLIC, CAMEROON, GABON, CONGO, DEMOCRATIC REPUBLIC OF THE CONGO, UGANDA, KENYA, RWANDA, BURUNDI, TANZANIA, ANGOLA, ZAMBIA, MALAWI, MOZAMBIQUE, ZIMBABWE, NAMIBIA, BOTSWANA, MADAGASCAR, MAURITIUS, COMOROS, SEYCHELLES, SWAZILAND, LESOTHO, REP. OF SOUTH AFRICA

RUSSIAN FEDERATION, KAZAKHSTAN, UZBEKISTAN, GEORGIA, ARMENIA, AZERBAIJAN, TURKMENISTAN, TAJIKISTAN, KYRGYZSTAN, MONGOLIA, IRAN, AFGHANISTAN, KUWAIT, BAHRAIN, QATAR, U.A.E., OMAN, PAKISTAN, NEPAL, BHUTAN, INDIA, BANGLADESH, MYANMAR (BURMA), CHINA, NORTH KOREA, SOUTH KOREA, JAPAN, LAOS, VIETNAM, THAILAND, CAMBODIA, PHILIPPINES, SRI LANKA, MALDIVES, BRUNEI, MALAYSIA, SINGAPORE, INDONESIA, PALAU, EAST TIMOR, PAPUA NEW GUINEA, FED. STATES OF MICRONESIA, MARSHALL ISLANDS, NAURU, KIRIBATI, SOLOMON ISLANDS, TUVALU, SAMOA, VANUATU, FIJI, AUSTRALIA

Poverty headcount ratio at $2 a day
(% of population, PPP)

2002
2008

Region	2002	2008
East Asia & Pacific	51.9	33.2
Europe & Central Asia	7.9	2.2
Latin America & Caribbean	22.2	12.4
Middle East & North Africa	19.7	13.9
South Asia	77.4	70.9
Sub-Saharan Africa	76.1	69.2

Average daily income of the population below $1.25 poverty line

Latin America & Caribbean
Sub-Saharan Africa
Other developing countries

(Dollars, PPP)

0.9
0.8
0.7
0.6
0.5
0.4
0.3
0.2
0.1
0

1981   1990   2005

69

Employment

Employment stability is the core of a stable economy but as economies change and develop, so must employment structure. Unpaid family work features strongly in the economy of many nations and this dependency lessens as nations develop. One indicator of a developed country is an increase of the proportion of the workforce employed in services such as finance, the media, retail and tourism.

However, development brings further employment challenges so that unemployment, youth unemployment, training and the employment of women are all issues remaining high in priority on political agendas, especially in the developed world.

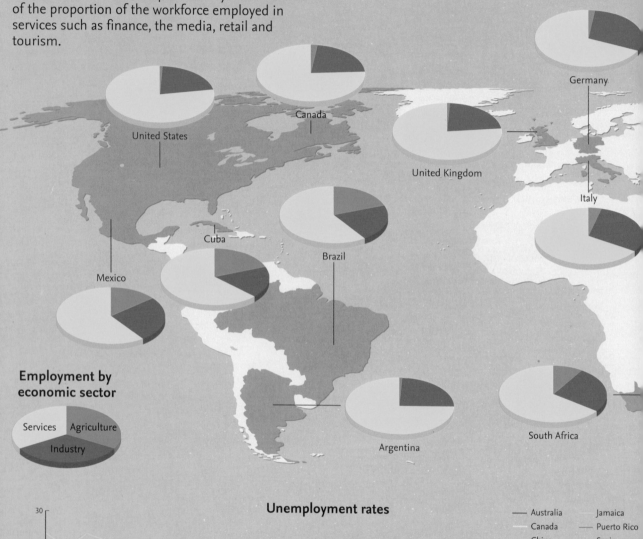

Germany

Canada

United States

United Kingdom

Italy

Cuba

Brazil

Mexico

South Africa

Employment by economic sector

Services
Agriculture
Industry

Argentina

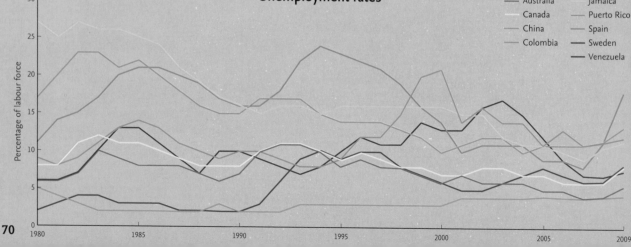

Unemployment rates

Percentage of labour force

—— Australia
—— Canada
—— China
—— Colombia

Jamaica
—— Puerto Rico
—— Spain
—— Sweden
—— Venezuela

1980 1985 1990 1995 2000 2005 2009

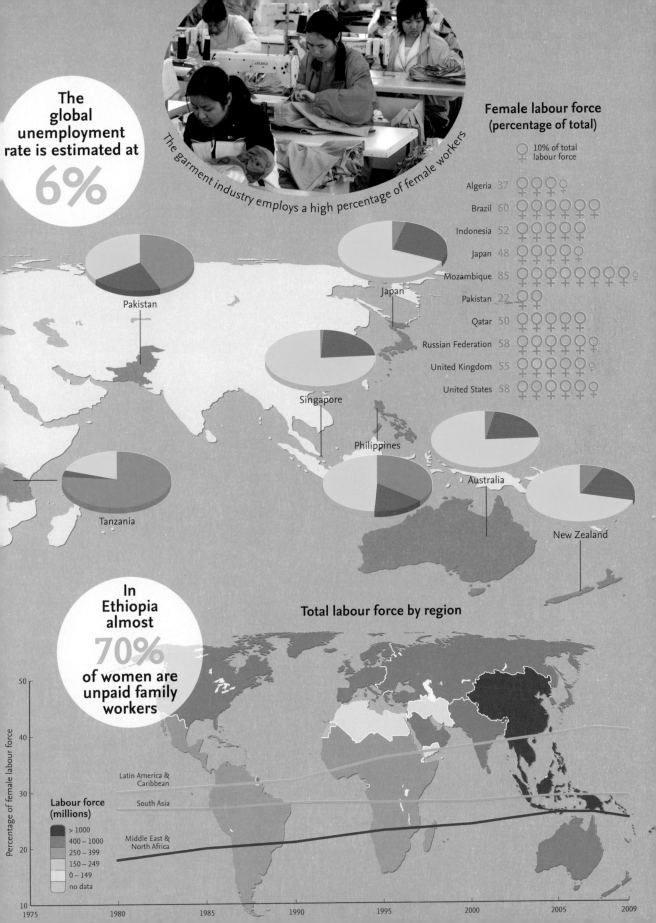

The garment industry employs a high percentage of female workers

The global unemployment rate is estimated at 6%

Female labour force
(percentage of total)

○ 10% of total labour force

Algeria	37	
Brazil	60	
Indonesia	52	
Japan	48	
Mozambique	85	
Pakistan	22	
Qatar	50	
Russian Federation	58	
United Kingdom	55	
United States	58	

Pakistan

Japan

Singapore

Philippines

Australia

Tanzania

New Zealand

In Ethiopia almost 70% of women are unpaid family workers

Total labour force by region

Percentage of female labour force

Latin America & Caribbean

South Asia

Middle East & North Africa

Labour force (millions)
- \> 1000
- 400 – 1000
- 250 – 399
- 150 – 249
- 0 – 149
- no data

10 20 30 40 50

1975 1980 1985 1990 1995 2000 2005 2009

Communications

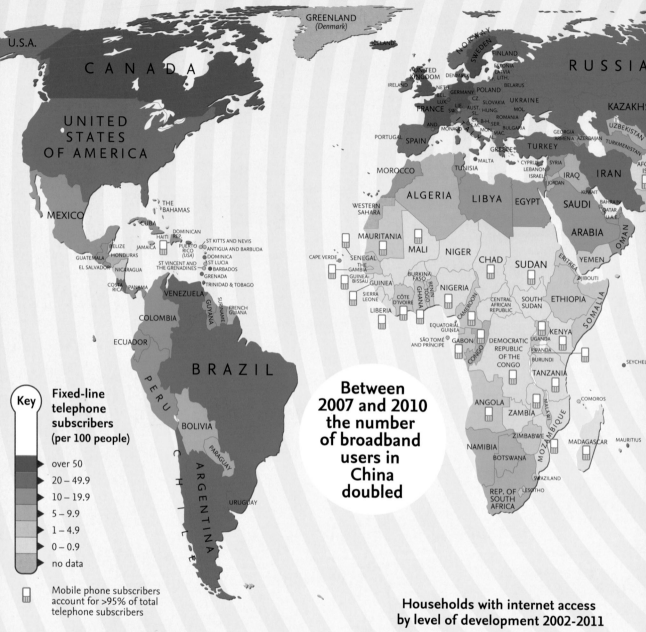

Key

Fixed-line telephone subscribers (per 100 people)

- over 50
- 20 – 49.9
- 10 – 19.9
- 5 – 9.9
- 1 – 4.9
- 0 – 0.9
- no data

Mobile phone subscribers account for >95% of total telephone subscribers

Between 2007 and 2010 the number of broadband users in China doubled

Infrastructure services, including information and communications technology, are the backbone of a functioning economy, facilitating growth and binding communities together. The Internet delivers information to schools and hospitals, and computers improve public and private services and increase productivity and participation. Increased computer usage and Internet access undoubtedly reduces the communications divide and plays a key part in the concept of globalization, but it can also be perceived as a threat to the identity of local cultures and economies.

Households with internet access by level of development 2002-2011

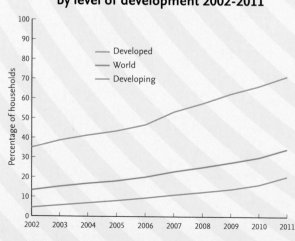

Percentage of households

- Developed
- World
- Developing

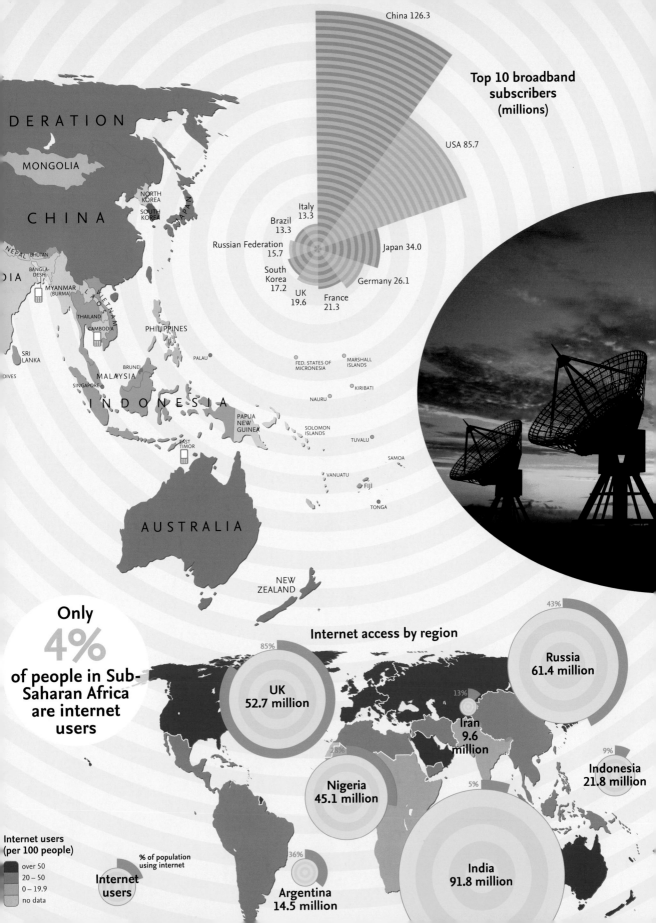

China 126.3

Top 10 broadband subscribers (millions)

USA 85.7

Italy 13.3

Brazil 13.3

Russian Federation 15.7

Japan 34.0

South Korea 17.2

Germany 26.1

UK 19.6

France 21.3

DERATION

MONGOLIA

CHINA

NORTH KOREA

SOUTH KOREA

JAPAN

NEPAL

BHUTAN

BANGLA-DESH

MYANMAR (BURMA)

LAOS

VIETNAM

THAILAND

CAMBODIA

PHILIPPINES

SRI LANKA

DIVES

BRUNEI

MALAYSIA

SINGAPORE

INDONESIA

PALAU

FED. STATES OF MICRONESIA

MARSHALL ISLANDS

KIRIBATI

NAURU

PAPUA NEW GUINEA

SOLOMON ISLANDS

TUVALU

EAST TIMOR

SAMOA

VANUATU

FIJI

AUSTRALIA

TONGA

NEW ZEALAND

Only **4%** of people in Sub-Saharan Africa are internet users

Internet access by region

85%

UK 52.7 million

43%

Russia 61.4 million

13%

Iran 9.6 million

9%

Indonesia 21.8 million

Nigeria 45.1 million

5%

India 91.8 million

36%

Argentina 14.5 million

Internet users (per 100 people)

over 50

20 – 50

0 – 19.9

no data

% of population using internet

Internet users

Aid

The global economy has become more integrated. Countries are exchanging more goods and services, and international financial flows have increased. Even in an expanding world economy, many countries cannot finance their own development. Aid helps to fill the gap. The provision of aid may take many forms – it may provide direct debt relief, it may give technical expertise or humanitarian assistance in times of disaster or it may provide finance for long-term development. In all cases the aim is for donor countries to help recipient countries build the capacity for change and for recipient countries to invest in their people and create an environment that sustains growth.

The top 4 donors contribute **>1/2** of world aid

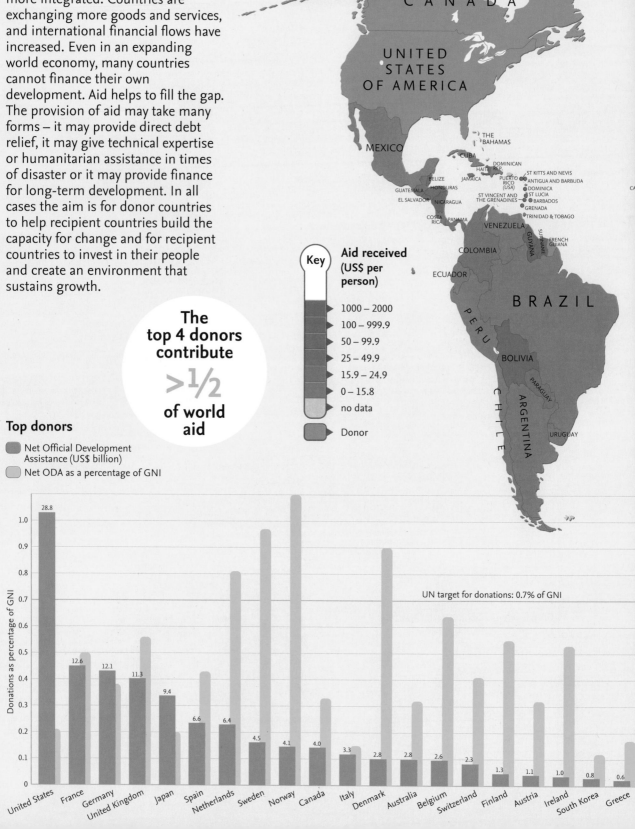

Key

Aid received (US$ per person)

- 1000 – 2000
- 100 – 999.9
- 50 – 99.9
- 25 – 49.9
- 15.9 – 24.9
- 0 – 15.8
- no data
- Donor

Top donors

- Net Official Development Assistance (US$ billion)
- Net ODA as a percentage of GNI

UN target for donations: 0.7% of GNI

Donations as percentage of GNI

Country	Net ODA (US$ billion)
United States	28.8
France	12.6
Germany	12.1
United Kingdom	11.3
Japan	9.4
Spain	6.6
Netherlands	6.4
Sweden	4.5
Norway	4.1
Canada	4.0
Italy	3.3
Denmark	2.8
Australia	2.8
Belgium	2.6
Switzerland	2.3
Finland	1.3
Austria	1.1
Ireland	1.0
South Korea	0.8
Greece	0.6

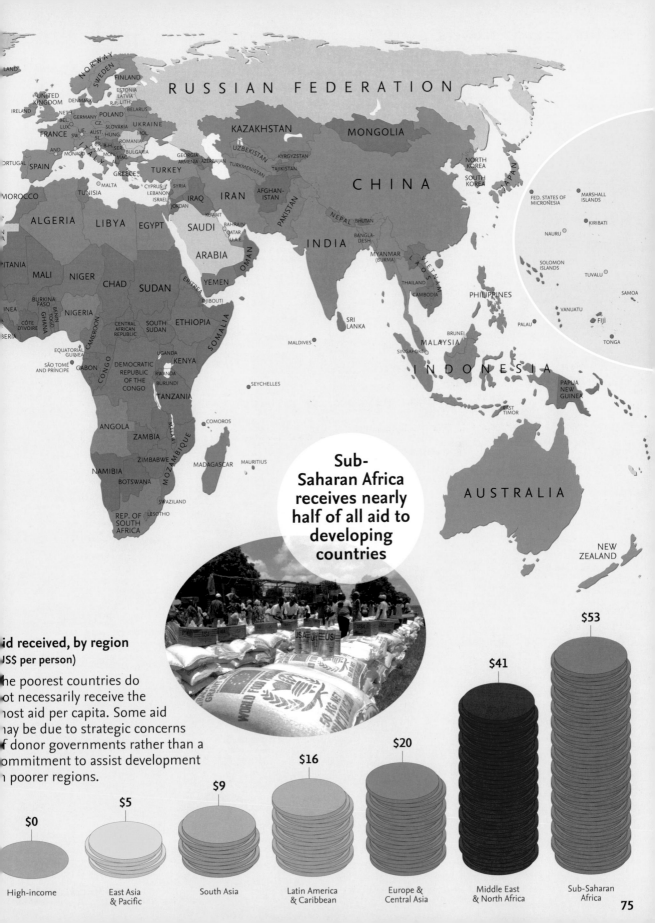

RUSSIAN FEDERATION

NORWAY
SWEDEN
FINLAND

UNITED
KINGDOM
IRELAND
DENMARK
LATVIA
ESTONIA
R.F. LITH.
BELARUS

FRANCE
GERMANY POLAND
BEL.
LUX.
CZ. SLOVAKIA UKRAINE
AUST. HUNG.
SW. SL. ROMANIA
AND. SER. BULGARIA
MONACO MON. MAC.
B-H.
M.
PORTUGAL
SPAIN

KAZAKHSTAN

MONGOLIA

ITALY
GREECE
TURKEY

GEORGIA
ARMENIA AZERBAIJAN
UZBEKISTAN
KYRGYZSTAN
TURKMENISTAN
TAJIKISTAN

NORTH
KOREA
SOUTH
KOREA

JAPAN

MOROCCO
TUNISIA
MALTA
CYPRUS
LEBANON
ISRAEL

SYRIA
IRAQ
IRAN
AFGHAN-
ISTAN

CHINA

FED. STATES OF
MICRONESIA
MARSHALL
ISLANDS

JORDAN
KUWAIT
BAHRAIN
QATAR
U.A.E.

PAKISTAN
NEPAL BHUTAN

NAURU
KIRIBATI

ALGERIA
LIBYA
EGYPT
SAUDI
ARABIA
OMAN
YEMEN

INDIA
BANGLA-
DESH

MYANMAR
(BURMA)
LAOS
VIETNAM

SOLOMON
ISLANDS
TUVALU
SAMOA

ITANIA
MALI
NIGER
CHAD
SUDAN
ERITREA
DJIBOUTI

THAILAND
CAMBODIA

VANUATU
FIJI

PALAU
TONGA

INEA
BURKINA
FASO
TOGO
GHANA
NIGERIA
CAMEROON
CENTRAL
AFRICAN
REPUBLIC
SOUTH
SUDAN
ETHIOPIA
SOMALIA

SRI
LANKA
MALDIVES

PHILIPPINES

BRUNEI

BENIN
CÔTE
D'IVOIRE
ERIA

EQUATORIAL
GUINEA
SÃO TOMÉ
AND PRÍNCIPE
GABON
CONGO
DEMOCRATIC
REPUBLIC
OF THE
CONGO
UGANDA
RWANDA
BURUNDI
KENYA

MALAYSIA
SINGAPORE

INDONESIA

PAPUA
NEW
GUINEA

TANZANIA
SEYCHELLES

EAST
TIMOR

ANGOLA
ZAMBIA
MOZAMBIQUE
MALAWI
COMOROS

ZIMBABWE
MADAGASCAR
MAURITIUS

NAMIBIA
BOTSWANA

SWAZILAND

REP. OF
SOUTH
AFRICA
LESOTHO

AUSTRALIA

NEW
ZEALAND

Sub-Saharan Africa receives nearly half of all aid to developing countries

id received, by region

(US$ per person)

he poorest countries do ot necessarily receive the ost aid per capita. Some aid ay be due to strategic concerns f donor governments rather than a ommitment to assist development n poorer regions.

$0	$5	$9	$16	$20	$41	$53
High-income	East Asia & Pacific	South Asia	Latin America & Caribbean	Europe & Central Asia	Middle East & North Africa	Sub-Saharan Africa

Aid Donors and Receivers

Sweden Austri
Denmark Sp
France S
United Thailand
Australia Slovenia
Luxembourg Japa
Slovakia Iceland
United K
Turkey
Norway Hungary U
Poland Gr

Donors
(Names are proportional to the value of aid donated)

Recipients

AFGHANISTAN	203.7
ALBANIA	113.4
ALGERIA	9.1
ANGOLA	12.9
ANTIGUA AND BARBUDA	67.8
ARGENTINA	3.2
ARMENIA	171.1
AZERBAIJAN	26.5
BANGLADESH	7.6
BARBADOS	47.7
BELARUS	10.1
BELIZE	83.6
BENIN	76.4
BHUTAN	179.9
BOLIVIA	73.6
BOSNIA-HERZEGOVINA	110.2
BOTSWANA	143.4
BRAZIL	1.7
BURKINA FASO	68.8
BURUNDI	66.1
CAMBODIA	48.8
CAMEROON	33.3
CAPE VERDE	**387.5**
CENTRAL AFRICAN REPUBLIC	53.6
CHAD	50.1
CHILE	4.7
CHINA	0.9
COLOMBIA	23.2
COMOROS	76.8
CONGO	76.8
CONGO, DEM REP OF THE	35.6
COSTA RICA	23.9
CÔTE D'IVOIRE	112.3
CROATIA	38.2
CUBA	10.4
DJIBOUTI	187.7
DOMINICA	**492.3**
DOMINICAN REPUBLIC	11.9
EAST TIMOR	191.2
ECUADOR	15.3
EGYPT	11.1
EL SALVADOR	44.9
EQUATORIAL GUINEA	46.7
ERITREA	28.5
ETHIOPIA	46.1
FIJI	83.7
GABON	52.6
GAMBIA, THE	75.1
GEORGIA	213.1
GHANA	66.4
GRENADA	**463.3**
GUATEMALA	26.8
GUINEA	21.3
GUINEA-BISSAU	90.3
GUYANA	227.5
HAITI	111.6
HONDURAS	61.2
INDIA	2.1
INDONESIA	4.6
IRAN	1.3
IRAQ	88.6
JAMAICA	55.4
JORDAN	127.8
KAZAKHSTAN	18.7
KENYA	44.7
KIRIBATI	277.2
KOSOVO	**436.5**
KYRGYZSTAN	59.1

Top 10 recipient for 2009 in Bo
(figures in millions of US $)

New Zealand

Netherlands

in Israel Belgium

itzerland Italy

South Korea

States

Germany

Finland Canada

ngdom

ted Arab Emirates

ce Portugal Czech Republic

131 billion US$ 2010, total Official Development Assistance (ODA)

MADAGASCAR	22.7
MALAWI	50.6
MALAYSIA	5.2
MALDIVES	107.5
MALI	75.7
MARSHALL ISLANDS	**963.2**
MAURITANIA	87.1
MAURITIUS	122
MEXICO	1.7
MICRONESIA, FED STATES OF	**1092.7**
MOLDOVA	68
MONGOLIA	139.4
MONTENEGRO	120.8
MOROCCO	28.5
MOZAMBIQUE	87.9
MYANMAR (BURMA)	7.1
NAMIBIA	150.2
NEPAL	29.1
NICARAGUA	134.8
NIGER	30.7
NIGERIA	10.7
NORTH KOREA	2.8
OMAN	74.5
PAKISTAN	16.4
PALAU	**1733**
PANAMA	19
PAPUA NEW GUINEA	61.4
PARAGUAY	23.4
PERU	15.2
PHILIPPINES	3.4
RWANDA	93.5
ST KITTS AND NEVIS	110.9
ST LUCIA	238.7
ST VINCENT AND THE GRENADINES	285.1
SAMOA	**432.9**
SÃO TOMÉ AND PRÍNCIPE	188.7
SENEGAL	81.2
SERBIA	83.1
SEYCHELLES	263.7
SIERRA LEONE	76.8
SOLOMON ISLANDS	**393.6**
SOMALIA	72.4
SOUTH AFRICA	21.8
SRI LANKA	34.7
SUDAN	54.1
SURINAME	302.2
SWAZILAND	48.9
SYRIA	11.6
TAJIKISTAN	58.8
TANZANIA	67.1
THAILAND	-1.1
TOGO	75.4
TONGA	380
TRINIDAD AND TOBAGO	5.2
TUNISIA	45.4
TURKEY	18.2
TURKMENISTAN	7.8
UGANDA	54.6
UKRAINE	14.5
URUGUAY	15.1
UZBEKISTAN	6.9
VANUATU	**430.8**
VENEZUELA	2.4
VIETNAM	42.9
YEMEN	21.2
ZAMBIA	98.1
ZIMBABWE	58.8

ENVIRONMENT

Environment and Development

Over the next few decades most population growth will take place in cities and urban areas. Although the rate of growth in many countries is falling, the absolute number will continue to increase for the foreseeable future. Developing urban areas are focal points for many environmental and health hazards. Issues such as solid waste disposal, provision of safe water and sanitation will determine the quality of the future urban environment.

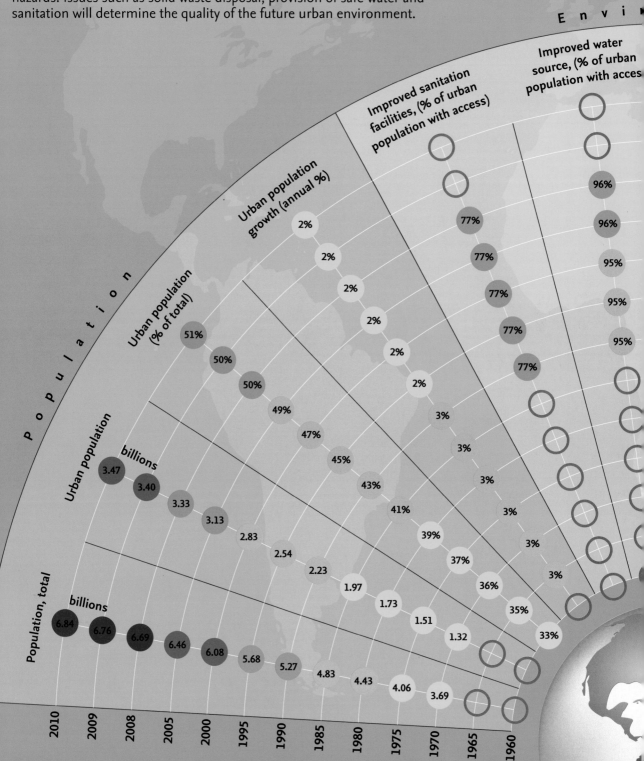

Improved water source, (% of urban population with access)

96%
96%
95%
95%
95%

Improved sanitation facilities, (% of urban population with access)

77%
77%
77%
77%
77%

Urban population growth (annual %)

2%
2%
2%
2%
2%
2%
3%
3%
3%
3%
3%
3%
3%

Urban population (% of total)

51%
50%
50%
49%
47%
45%
43%
41%
39%
37%
36%
35%
33%

Population

Urban population

billions

3.47
3.40
3.33
3.13
2.83
2.54
2.23
1.97
1.73
1.51
1.32

Population, total

billions

6.84
6.76
6.69
6.46
6.08
5.68
5.27
4.83
4.43
4.06
3.69

2010
2009
2008
2005
2000
1995
1990
1985
1980
1975
1970
1965
1960

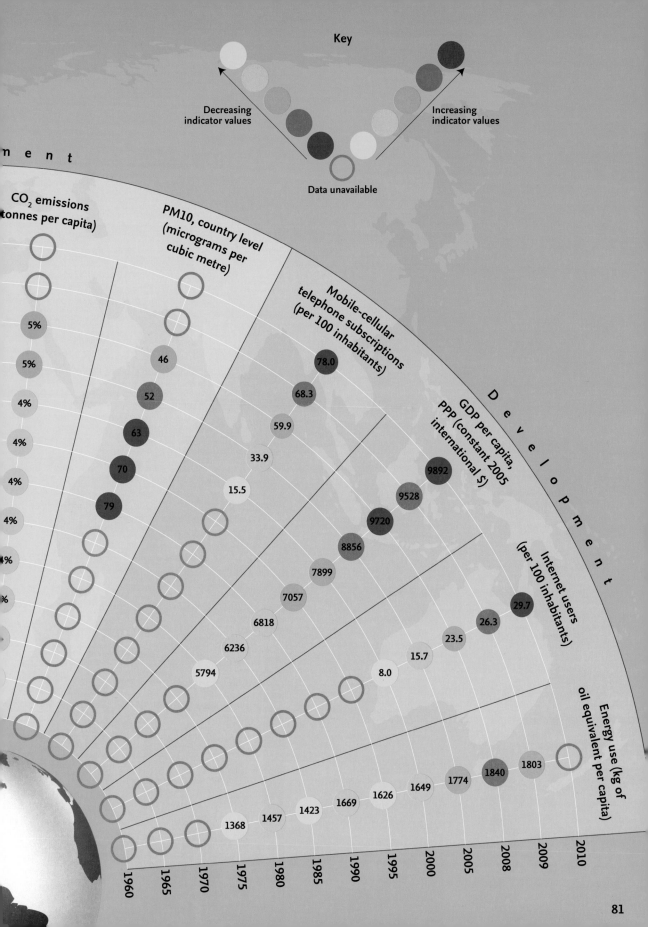

Key

Decreasing indicator values

Increasing indicator values

Data unavailable

m e n t

CO₂ emissions (tonnes per capita)

PM10, country level (micrograms per cubic metre)

Mobile-cellular telephone subscriptions (per 100 inhabitants)

GDP per capita, PPP (constant 2005 international $)

Internet users (per 100 inhabitants)

Energy use (kg of oil equivalent per capita)

D e v e l o p m e n t

CO₂ emissions: 5%, 5%, 4%, 4%, 4%, 4%, 4%, 4%

PM10: 46, 52, 63, 70, 79

Mobile-cellular telephone subscriptions: 78.0, 68.3, 59.9, 33.9, 15.5

GDP per capita: 9892, 9528, 9720, 8856, 7899, 7057, 6818, 6236, 5794

Internet users: 29.7, 26.3, 23.5, 15.7, 8.0

Energy use: 1803, 1840, 1774, 1649, 1626, 1669, 1423, 1457, 1368

Years: 1960, 1965, 1970, 1975, 1980, 1985, 1990, 1995, 2000, 2005, 2008, 2009, 2010

81

Physical World

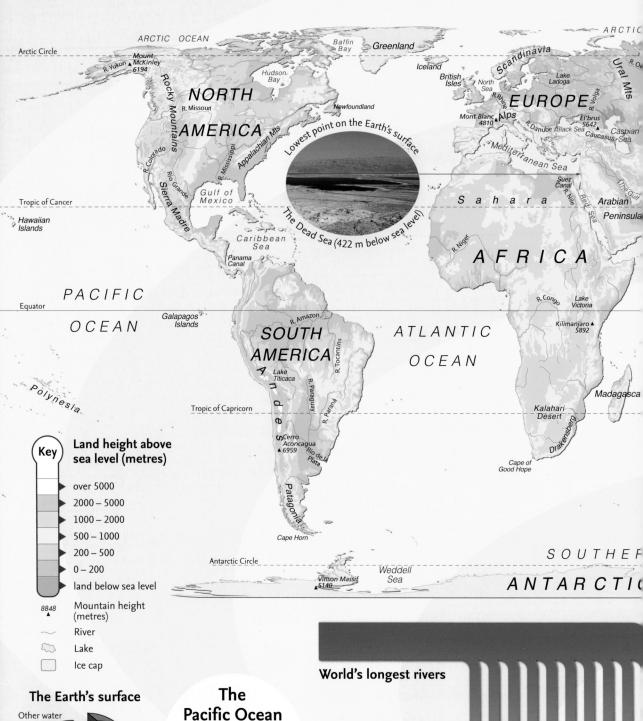

ARCTIC OCEAN

Arctic Circle

Baffin Bay
Greenland
Iceland
British Isles
North Sea
Scandinavia
Lake Ladoga
Ural Mts
R. Ob

Mount McKinley ▲ 6194
R. Yukon
Rocky Mountains

NORTH AMERICA

R. Missouri
Newfoundland

EUROPE
Mont Blanc ▲ 4810
Alps
R. Rhine
R. Volga
El'brus ▲ 5642
Caucasus
Caspian Sea
R. Danube
Black Sea

Lowest point on the Earth's surface

Mediterranean Sea
Suez Canal
R. Nile
The Gulf
Red Sea
Arabian Peninsula

Tropic of Cancer

R. Colorado
Rio Grande
Sierra Madre
Gulf of Mexico
R. Mississippi
Appalachian Mts

The Dead Sea (422 m below sea level)

S a h a r a

A F R I C A

Hawaiian Islands

Caribbean Sea
Panama Canal

R. Niger

PACIFIC

Equator

OCEAN

Galapagos Islands

R. Amazon

SOUTH AMERICA

A T L A N T I C
O C E A N

R. Congo
Lake Victoria
Kilimanjaro ▲ 5892

Lake Titicaca
R. Paraguay
R. Paraná
R. Tocantins

Polynesia

Madagascar

Tropic of Capricorn

A n d e s
Cerro Aconcagua ▲ 6959
Rio de la Plata

Kalahari Desert
Drakensberg

Cape of Good Hope

Patagonia

Cape Horn

Antarctic Circle

Weddell Sea

Vinson Massif ▲ 5140

SOUTHERN

ANTARCTICA

Key

Land height above sea level (metres)

- over 5000
- 2000 – 5000
- 1000 – 2000
- 500 – 1000
- 200 – 500
- 0 – 200
- land below sea level

8848 ▲ Mountain height (metres)

River

Lake

Ice cap

The Earth's surface

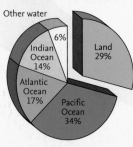

Other water 6%
Indian Ocean 14%
Atlantic Ocean 17%
Pacific Ocean 34%
Land 29%

The Pacific Ocean is nearly as large as all the other oceans put together

World's longest rivers

Mekong 4425km — ⑩
Río de la Plata-Paraná 4500km — ⑨
Congo 4667km — ⑧
Yellow (Huang He) 5464km — ⑦
Yenisey-Angara-Selenga 5500km — ⑥
Ob'-Irtysh 5568km — ⑤
Mississippi-Missouri 5969km — ④
Yangtze (Chang Jiang) 6380km — ③
Amazon 6516km — ②
Nile 6695km —

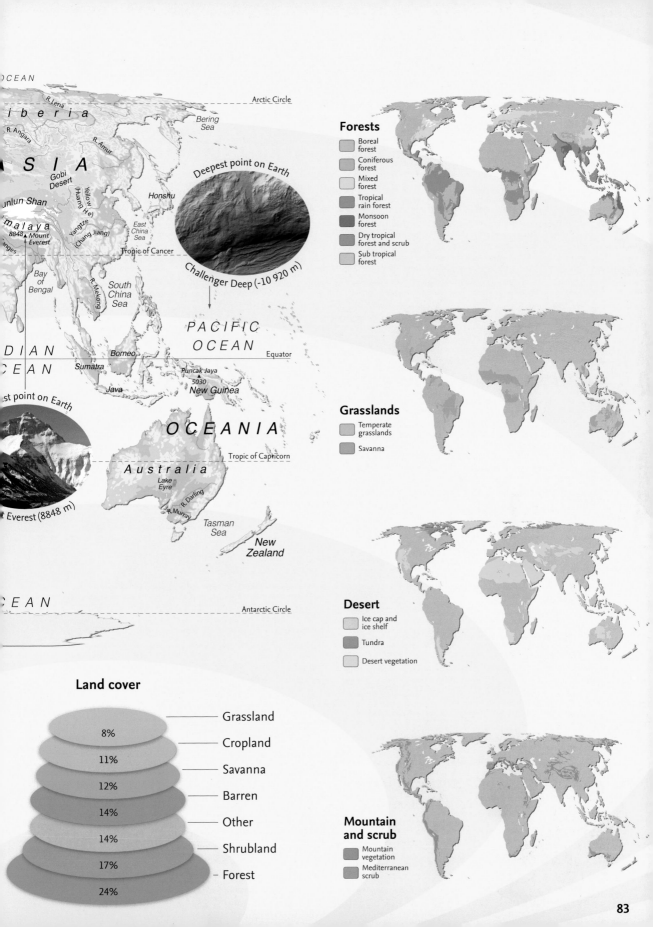

OCEAN

R. Lena

Arctic Circle

iberia

Bering
Sea

R. Angara

R. Amur

ASIA

Gobi
Desert

Honshu

unlun Shan

Yellow
(Huang He)

malaya

Yangtze
(Chang Jiang)

8848 Mount
Everest

East
China
Sea

Tropic of Cancer

anges

Bay
of
Bengal

R. Mekong

South
China
Sea

Deepest point on Earth

Challenger Deep (-10 920 m)

DIAN

CEAN

Sumatra

Borneo

Equator

Java

Puncak Jaya
5030
New Guinea

st point on Earth

OCEANIA

PACIFIC
OCEAN

Tropic of Capricorn

Australia

Lake
Eyre

R. Darling

t Everest (8848 m)

R. Murray

Tasman
Sea

New
Zealand

Antarctic Circle

OCEAN

Forests

- Boreal forest
- Coniferous forest
- Mixed forest
- Tropical rain forest
- Monsoon forest
- Dry tropical forest and scrub
- Sub tropical forest

Grasslands

- Temperate grasslands
- Savanna

Desert

- Ice cap and ice shelf
- Tundra
- Desert vegetation

Mountain and scrub

- Mountain vegetation
- Mediterranean scrub

Land cover

- 8% — Grassland
- 11% — Cropland
- 12% — Savanna
- 14% — Barren
- 14% — Other
- 17% — Shrubland
- 24% — Forest

Biomes of the World

A biome is a large area with geographic and climatic similarities as well as similar flora, fauna, and microorganisms. Species living in each biome are adapted to its varying conditions of water, heat and soil. Biomes are classified according to their predominant vegetation. The conservation and preservation of biomes is a major concern to us all.

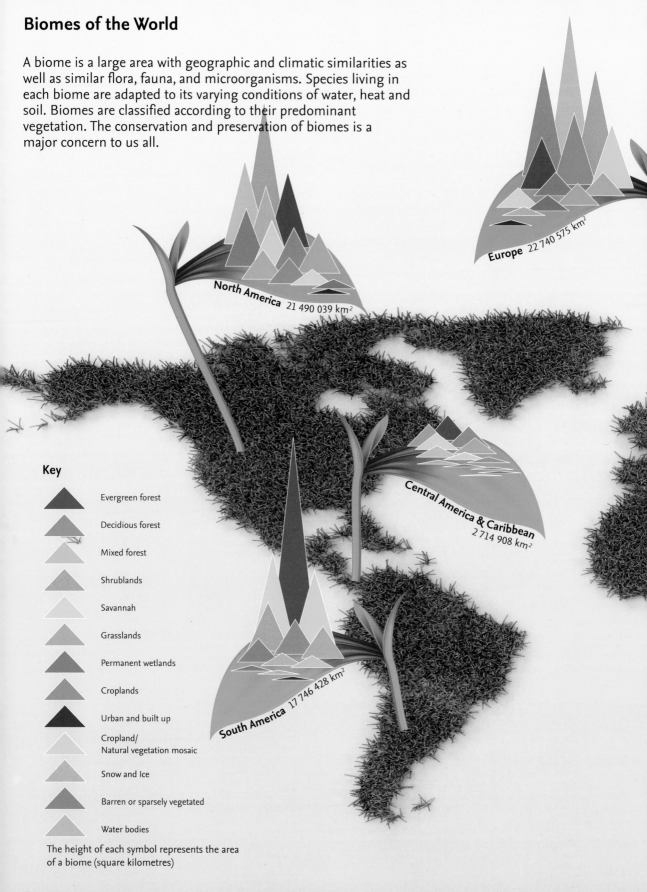

Europe 22 740 575 km²

North America 21 490 039 km²

Central America & Caribbean 2 714 908 km²

South America 17 746 428 km²

Key

- Evergreen forest
- Decidious forest
- Mixed forest
- Shrublands
- Savannah
- Grasslands
- Permanent wetlands
- Croplands
- Urban and built up
- Cropland/ Natural vegetation mosaic
- Snow and Ice
- Barren or sparsely vegetated
- Water bodies

The height of each symbol represents the area of a biome (square kilometres)

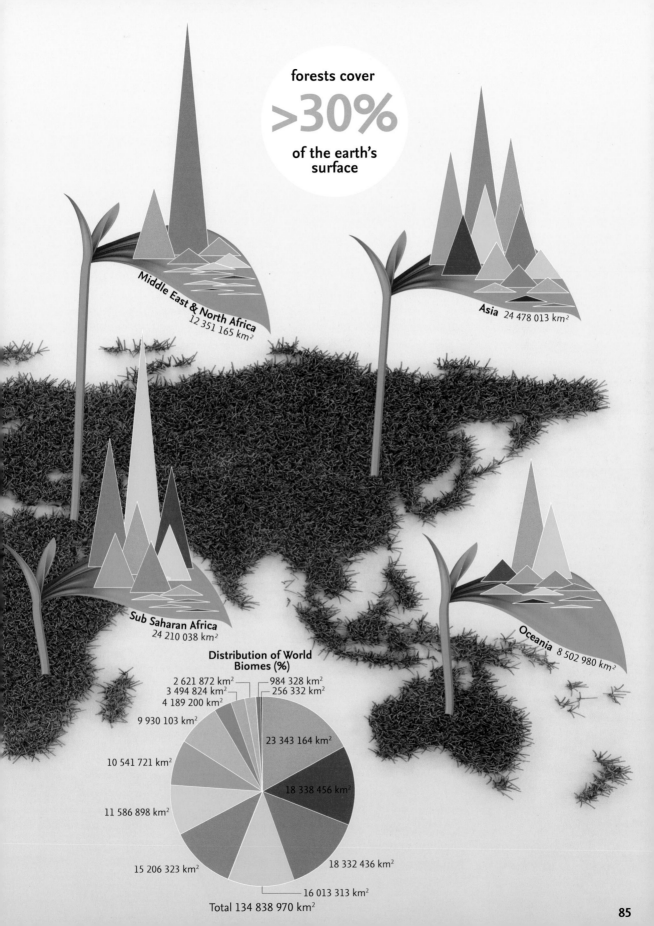

forests cover

>30%

of the earth's surface

Middle East & North Africa
12 351 165 km²

Asia 24 478 013 km²

Sub Saharan Africa
24 210 038 km²

Oceania 8 502 980 km²

Distribution of World Biomes (%)

2 621 872 km²   984 328 km²
3 494 824 km²   256 332 km²
4 189 200 km²

9 930 103 km²   23 343 164 km²

10 541 721 km²   18 338 456 km²

11 586 898 km²

15 206 323 km²   18 332 436 km²

16 013 313 km²

Total 134 838 970 km²

85

Environmental Issues and Pollution

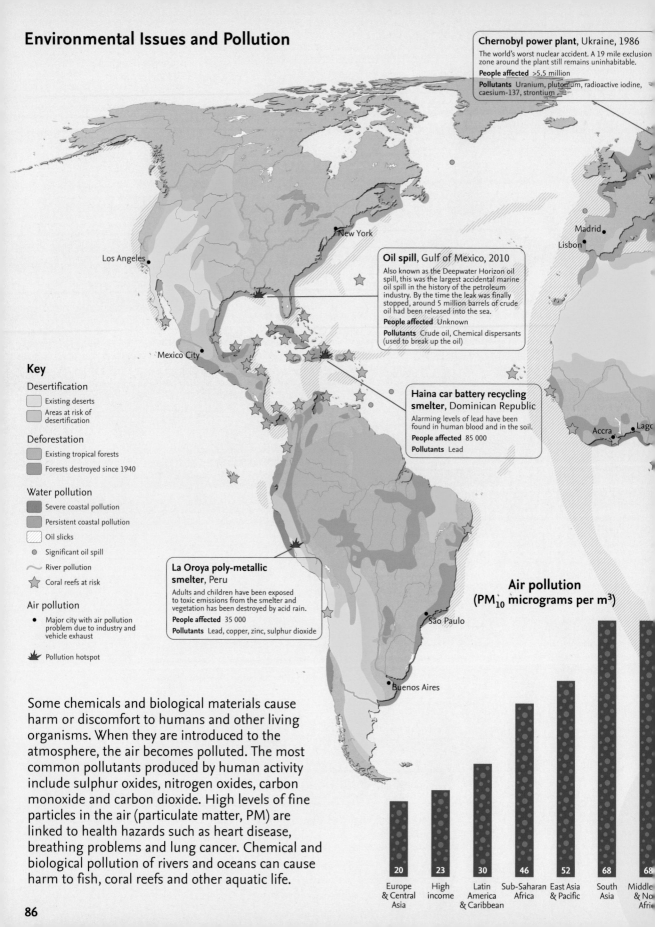

Chernobyl power plant, Ukraine, 1986
The world's worst nuclear accident. A 19 mile exclusion zone around the plant still remains uninhabitable.
People affected >5.5 million
Pollutants Uranium, plutonium, radioactive iodine, caesium-137, strontium

Oil spill, Gulf of Mexico, 2010
Also known as the Deepwater Horizon oil spill, this was the largest accidental marine oil spill in the history of the petroleum industry. By the time the leak was finally stopped, around 5 million barrels of crude oil had been released into the sea.
People affected Unknown
Pollutants Crude oil, Chemical dispersants (used to break up the oil)

Haina car battery recycling smelter, Dominican Republic
Alarming levels of lead have been found in human blood and in the soil.
People affected 85 000
Pollutants Lead

La Oroya poly-metallic smelter, Peru
Adults and children have been exposed to toxic emissions from the smelter and vegetation has been destroyed by acid rain.
People affected 35 000
Pollutants Lead, copper, zinc, sulphur dioxide

New York
Los Angeles
Madrid
Lisbon
Mexico City
Accra
Lago
São Paulo
Buenos Aires

Key

Desertification
- Existing deserts
- Areas at risk of desertification

Deforestation
- Existing tropical forests
- Forests destroyed since 1940

Water pollution
- Severe coastal pollution
- Persistent coastal pollution
- Oil slicks
- Significant oil spill
- River pollution
- Coral reefs at risk

Air pollution
- Major city with air pollution problem due to industry and vehicle exhaust
- Pollution hotspot

Air pollution
(PM_{10} micrograms per m^3)

Europe & Central Asia	High income	Latin America & Caribbean	Sub-Saharan Africa	East Asia & Pacific	South Asia	Middle East & No Afric
20	23	30	46	52	68	68

Some chemicals and biological materials cause harm or discomfort to humans and other living organisms. When they are introduced to the atmosphere, the air becomes polluted. The most common pollutants produced by human activity include sulphur oxides, nitrogen oxides, carbon monoxide and carbon dioxide. High levels of fine particles in the air (particulate matter, PM) are linked to health hazards such as heart disease, breathing problems and lung cancer. Chemical and biological pollution of rivers and oceans can cause harm to fish, coral reefs and other aquatic life.

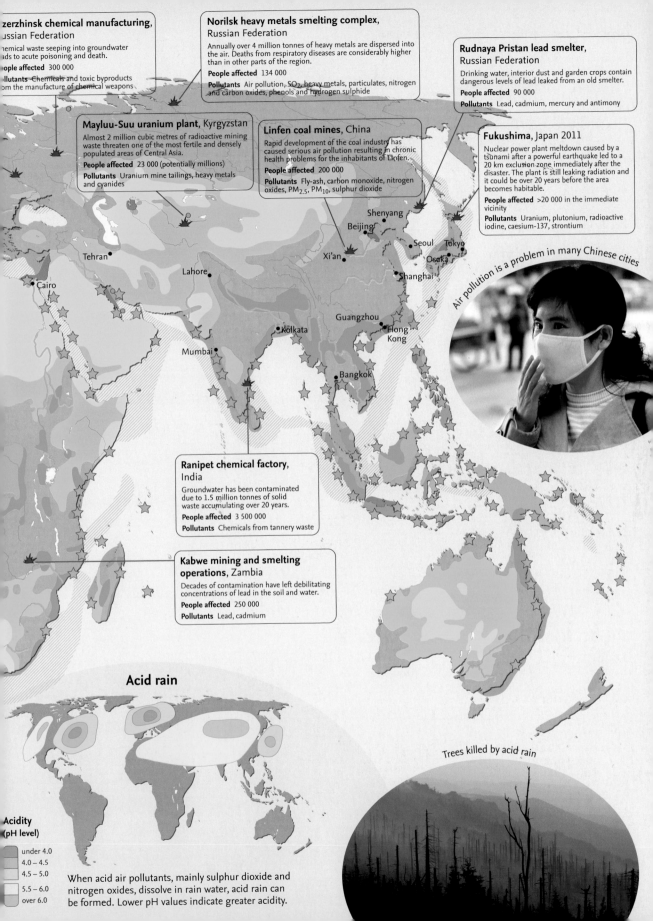

zerzhinsk chemical manufacturing,
russian Federation

hemical waste seeping into groundwater
ads to acute poisoning and death.

ople affected 300 000

llutants Chemicals and toxic byproducts
om the manufacture of chemical weapons

Norilsk heavy metals smelting complex,
Russian Federation

Annually over 4 million tonnes of heavy metals are dispersed into
the air. Deaths from respiratory diseases are considerably higher
than in other parts of the region.

People affected 134 000

Pollutants Air pollution, SO_2, heavy metals, particulates, nitrogen
and carbon oxides, phenols and hydrogen sulphide

Rudnaya Pristan lead smelter,
Russian Federation

Drinking water, interior dust and garden crops contain
dangerous levels of lead leaked from an old smelter.

People affected 90 000

Pollutants Lead, cadmium, mercury and antimony

Mayluu-Suu uranium plant, Kyrgyzstan

Almost 2 million cubic metres of radioactive mining
waste threaten one of the most fertile and densely
populated areas of Central Asia.

People affected 23 000 (potentially millions)

Pollutants Uranium mine tailings, heavy metals
and cyanides

Linfen coal mines, China

Rapid development of the coal industry has
caused serious air pollution resulting in chronic
health problems for the inhabitants of Linfen.

People affected 200 000

Pollutants Fly-ash, carbon monoxide, nitrogen
oxides, $PM_{2.5}$, PM_{10}, sulphur dioxide

Fukushima, Japan 2011

Nuclear power plant meltdown caused by a
tsunami after a powerful earthquake led to a
20 km exclusion zone immediately after the
disaster. The plant is still leaking radiation and
it could be over 20 years before the area
becomes habitable.

People affected >20 000 in the immediate
vicinity

Pollutants Uranium, plutonium, radioactive
iodine, caesium-137, strontium

Tehran

Shenyang

Beijing

Seoul

Tokyo

Xi'an

Osaka

Lahore

Shanghai

Cairo

Guangzhou

Kolkata

Hong
Kong

Mumbai

Bangkok

Air pollution is a problem in many Chinese cities

Ranipet chemical factory,
India

Groundwater has been contaminated
due to 1.5 million tonnes of solid
waste accumulating over 20 years.

People affected 3 500 000

Pollutants Chemicals from tannery waste

**Kabwe mining and smelting
operations,** Zambia

Decades of contamination have left debilitating
concentrations of lead in the soil and water.

People affected 250 000

Pollutants Lead, cadmium

Acid rain

Trees killed by acid rain

Acidity
(pH level)

under 4.0

4.0 – 4.5

4.5 – 5.0

5.5 – 6.0

over 6.0

When acid air pollutants, mainly sulphur dioxide and
nitrogen oxides, dissolve in rain water, acid rain can
be formed. Lower pH values indicate greater acidity.

Forest Change and Desertification

Forest area

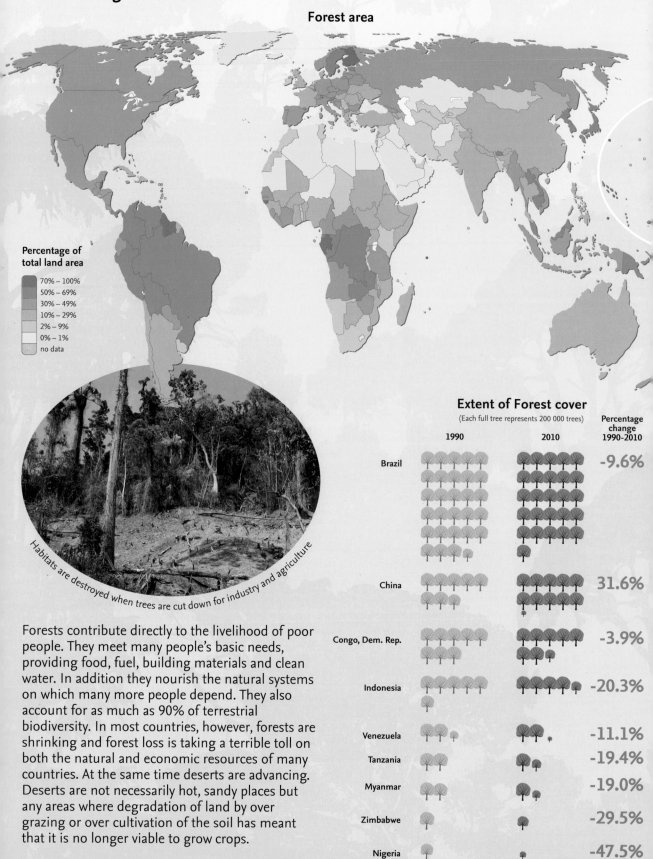

Percentage of total land area
- 70% – 100%
- 50% – 69%
- 30% – 49%
- 10% – 29%
- 2% – 9%
- 0% – 1%
- no data

Habitats are destroyed when trees are cut down for industry and agriculture

Extent of Forest cover

(Each full tree represents 200 000 trees)

	1990	2010	Percentage change 1990-2010
Brazil			-9.6%
China			31.6%
Congo, Dem. Rep.			-3.9%
Indonesia			-20.3%
Venezuela			-11.1%
Tanzania			-19.4%
Myanmar			-19.0%
Zimbabwe			-29.5%
Nigeria			-47.5%

Forests contribute directly to the livelihood of poor people. They meet many people's basic needs, providing food, fuel, building materials and clean water. In addition they nourish the natural systems on which many more people depend. They also account for as much as 90% of terrestrial biodiversity. In most countries, however, forests are shrinking and forest loss is taking a terrible toll on both the natural and economic resources of many countries. At the same time deserts are advancing. Deserts are not necessarily hot, sandy places but any areas where degradation of land by over grazing or over cultivation of the soil has meant that it is no longer viable to grow crops.

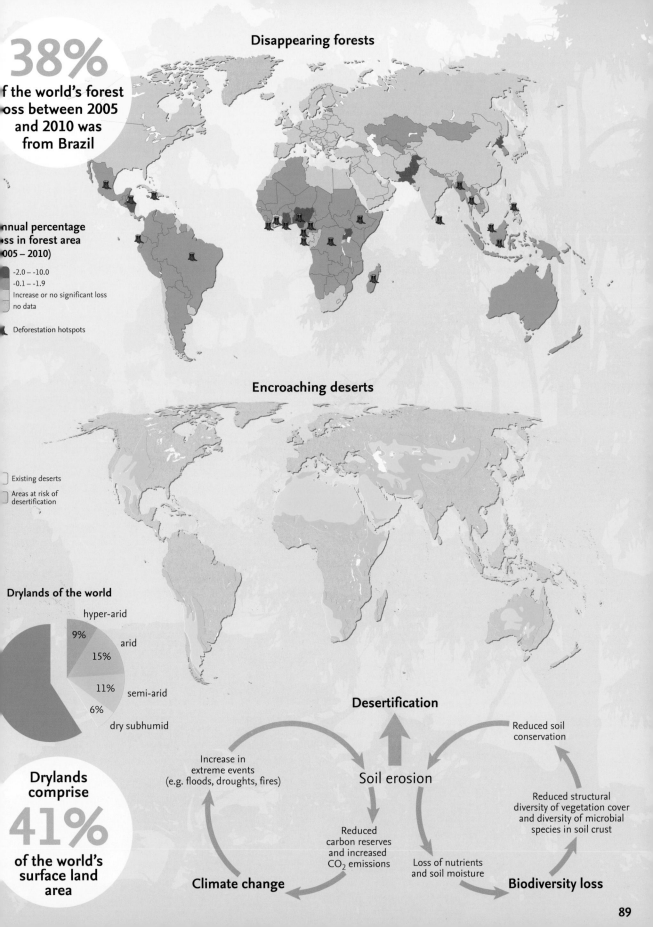

Disappearing forests

38%
f the world's forest
oss between 2005
and 2010 was
from Brazil

nnual percentage
oss in forest area
005 – 2010)

- -2.0 – -10.0
- -0.1 – -1.9
- Increase or no significant loss
- no data

🪵 Deforestation hotspots

Encroaching deserts

- Existing deserts
- Areas at risk of desertification

Drylands of the world

hyper-arid
9%
arid
15%
11%
semi-arid
6%
dry subhumid

Drylands comprise
41%
of the world's surface land area

Desertification

Soil erosion

Increase in extreme events (e.g. floods, droughts, fires)

Reduced carbon reserves and increased CO_2 emissions

Reduced soil conservation

Reduced structural diversity of vegetation cover and diversity of microbial species in soil crust

Loss of nutrients and soil moisture

Climate change

Biodiversity loss

Freshwater and Irrigation

Freshwater makes up only about 2.5% of the world's total water resources and most of this is locked up in permanent ice or snow or in deep groundwater aquifers. The provision of freshwater to dry areas that otherwise could not sustain human habitation or agricultural use is a major demand on the world's freshwater supply. 70% of global freshwater consumption is used in agriculture with most of this taken for irrigation. As the world needs to increase food production for a growing population, so the demand on freshwater for agricultural consumption will also grow.

Distribution of Global Water Resources

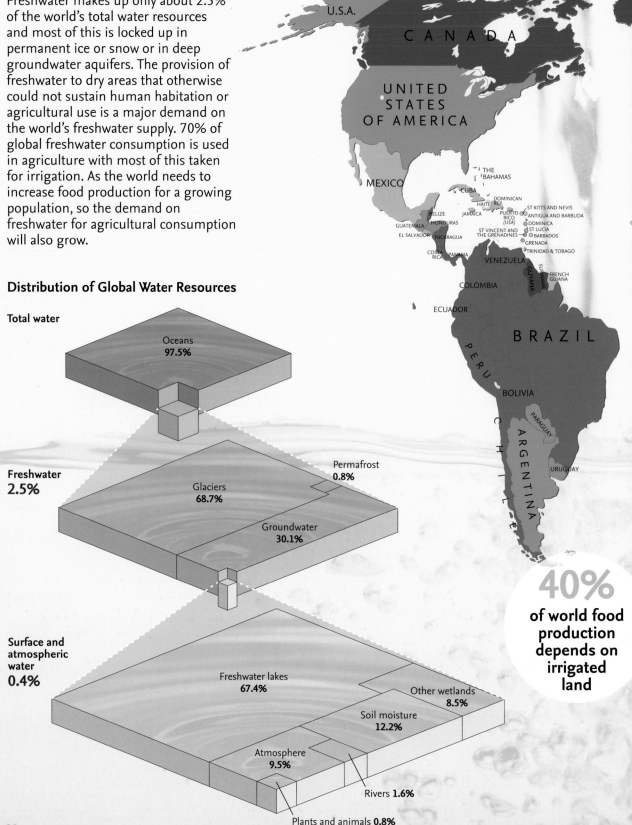

Total water

Oceans
97.5%

Freshwater
2.5%

Permafrost
0.8%

Glaciers
68.7%

Groundwater
30.1%

Surface and atmospheric water
0.4%

Freshwater lakes
67.4%

Other wetlands
8.5%

Soil moisture
12.2%

Atmosphere
9.5%

Rivers **1.6%**

Plants and animals **0.8%**

U.S.A.

C A N A D A

UNITED STATES OF AMERICA

MEXICO

THE BAHAMAS

CUBA

HAITI

DOMINICAN REP.

BELIZE

JAMAICA

PUERTO RICO (USA)

ST KITTS AND NEVIS

ANTIGUA AND BARBUDA

DOMINICA

ST LUCIA

GUATEMALA

HONDURAS

EL SALVADOR

NICARAGUA

ST VINCENT AND THE GRENADINES

BARBADOS

GRENADA

TRINIDAD & TOBAGO

COSTA RICA

PANAMA

VENEZUELA

COLOMBIA

ECUADOR

GUYANA

SURINAME

FRENCH GUIANA

B R A Z I L

P E R U

BOLIVIA

PARAGUAY

A R G E N T I N A

C H I L E

URUGUAY

GREEN

40%
of world food production depends on irrigated land

90

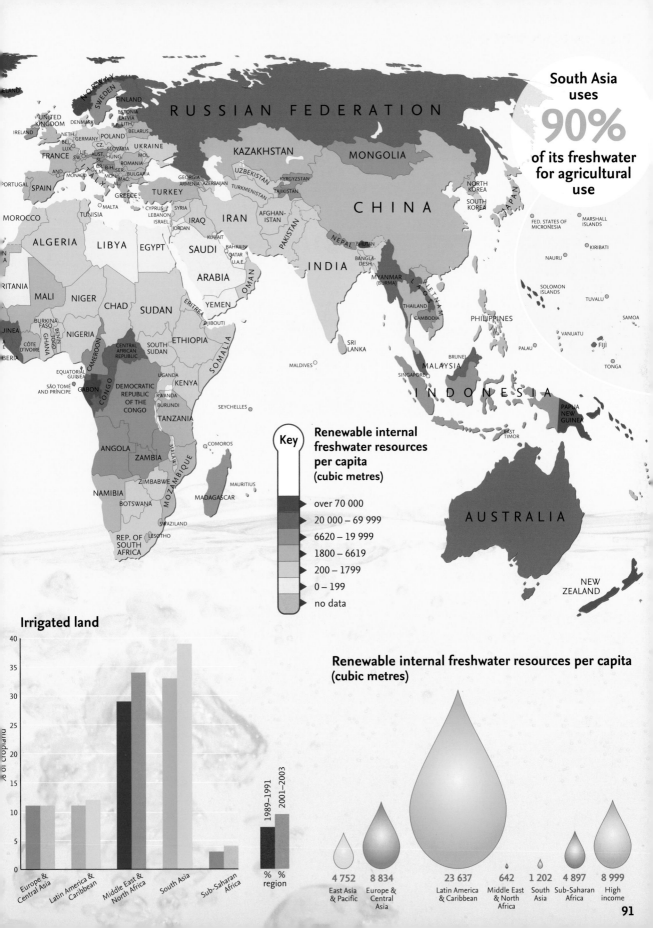

South Asia uses

90%

of its freshwater for agricultural use

Renewable internal freshwater resources per capita (cubic metres)

Key	
	over 70 000
	20 000 – 69 999
	6620 – 19 999
	1800 – 6619
	200 – 1799
	0 – 199
	no data

Irrigated land

% of cropland

1989–1991
2001–2003

Europe & Central Asia
Latin America & Caribbean
Middle East & North Africa
South Asia
Sub-Saharan Africa

% region

Renewable internal freshwater resources per capita (cubic metres)

4 752	8 834	23 637	642	1 202	4 897	8 999
East Asia & Pacific	Europe & Central Asia	Latin America & Caribbean	Middle East & North Africa	South Asia	Sub-Saharan Africa	High income

Water Withdrawals

Annual precipitation globally amounts to almost 110 000 km³. Most of this evaporates from the ground or transpires from vegetation. The remainder is converted to surface runoff and groundwater, described as renewable freshwater resources. Part of this water is being removed by installing infrastructure. This removal of water is called water withdrawal and most withdrawn water is returned to the environment after it has been used. The quality of the returned water may be less than the quality when it was originally removed. There are three types of water withdrawal: agricultural, municipal and industrial water withdrawal. At global level, 70 percent is withdrawn for agricultural, 11 percent for municipal and 19 percent for industrial use.

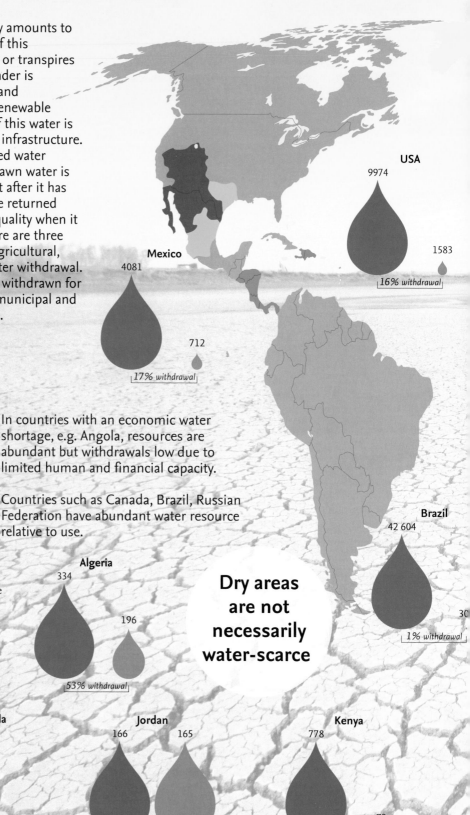

USA
9974
1583
16% withdrawal

Mexico
4081
712
17% withdrawal

Brazil
42 604
30
1% withdrawal

In countries with an economic water shortage, e.g. Angola, resources are abundant but withdrawals low due to limited human and financial capacity.

Countries such as Canada, Brazil, Russian Federation have abundant water resource relative to use.

Dry areas are not necessarily water-scarce

Key

Renewable water resources (m³ per capita)

Water withdrawal (m³ per capita)

% withdrawal

Water Scarcity

- extreme physical water shortage
- physical or approaching physical water shortage
- economic water shortage
- little or no water scarcity
- no data

Algeria
334
196
53% withdrawal

Angola
7976
43.02
0.5% withdrawal

Jordan
166
165
99% withdrawal

Kenya
778
73
9% withdrawal

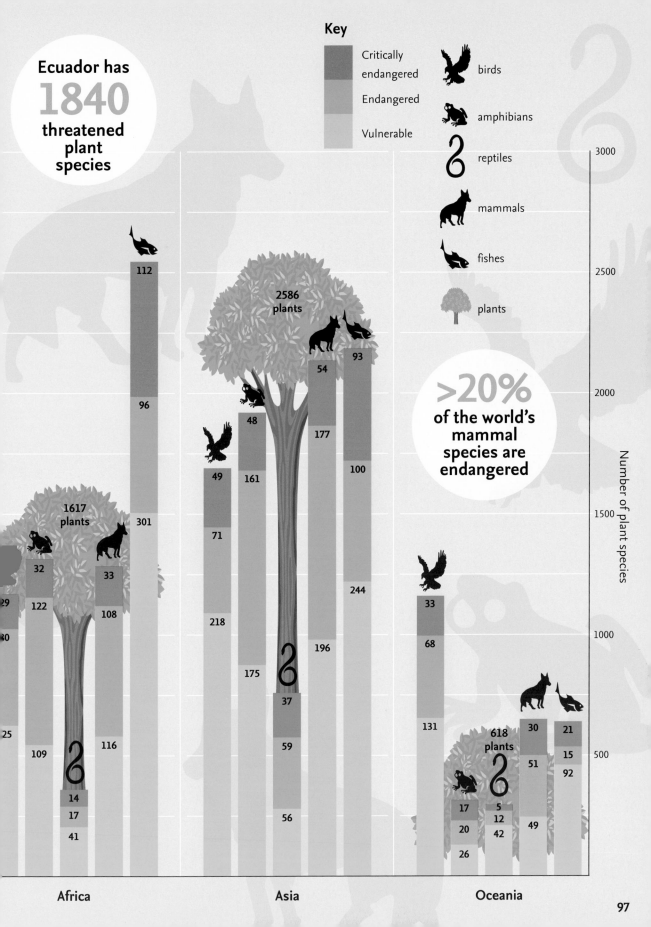

Key

Critically endangered

Endangered

Vulnerable

birds

amphibians

reptiles

mammals

fishes

plants

Ecuador has **1840** threatened plant species

>20% of the world's mammal species are endangered

Number of plant species

3000

2500

2000

1500

1000

500

Africa

1617 plants

112
96
301

32
122
29
30
25
109
14
17
41

33
108
116

Asia

2586 plants

49
71
218
175

48
161
37
59
56

54
177
100
244
196

93

Oceania

618 plants

33
68
131

17
20
26

5
12
42

30
51
49

21
15
92

97

Animal Survival

Name Polar Bear   **Class** Mammalia
Scientific *Ursus maritimus*   **Order** Carnivore

Population The estimated number of polar bears in the wild is 20-50 thousand

Biogeographical region Within the Arctic Circle; Canada; Greenland; Norway; Russian Federation; Alaska (U.S.A.)

Name Asian Elephant   **Class** Mammalia
Scientific *Elephas maximus*   **Order** Herbivore

Population The estimated Asian elephant population is 40-50 thousand

Biogeographical region Bangladesh; Bhutan; Cambodia; China; India; Laos; Malaysia; Myanmar; Nepal; Sri Lanka; Thailand; Vietnam

Name Southern Bluefin Tuna   **Class** Actinopterygii
Scientific *Thunnus maccoyii*   **Order** Omnivore

Population There has been an estimated 85% decline in spawning stock from 1973 to 2009

Biogeographical region Argentina; Australia; Brazil; Indonesia; Madagascar; New Zealand; South Africa; Southern Indian Ocean

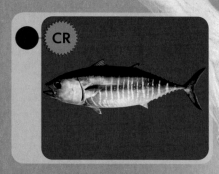

Name Mountain Gorilla   **Class** Mammalia
Scientific *Gorilla beringei*   **Order** Omnivore

Population 2010 Estimated total population worldwide is 790

Biogeographical region Democratic Republic of the Congo; Rwanda; Uganda

Name Giant Panda   **Class** Mammalia
Scientific *Ailuropoda melanoleuea*   **Order** Carnivore

Population Total wild population is estimated at 1-2 thousand

Biogeographical region South Central China

Name Leatherback Turtle   **Class** Reptilia
Scientific *Dermochelys coriacea*   **Order** Omnivore

Population 26-43 thousand
Biogeographical region Worldwide

Name Tiger   **Class** Mammalia
Scientific *Panthera tigris*   **Order** Carnivore

Population Around 4000 tigers remain in the wild
Biogeographical region Bangladesh; Bhutan; Cambodia; China; India; Indonesia; Laos; Malaysia; Myanmar; Nepal; Russian Federation; Thailand; Vietnam

Name Blue-throated Macaw   **Class** Aves
Scientific *Ava glaucogulavis*   **Order** -

Population It is estimated that 250 remain
Biogeographical region Northern Bolivia

Name Magellanic Penguin   **Class** Aves
Scientific *Spheniscoformes*   **Order** Carnivore

Population The world wide estimate is 1300 pairs
Biogeographical region Argentina; Chile; Falkland Islands; Brazil; Uruguay

11 out of the 18 penguin species are experiencing population decreases

Threats

- Climate change
- Global warming
- Habitat degradation
- Habitat fragmentation
- Habitat loss
- Unsustainable fishing practices
- Poaching
- Disease
- Pollution
- Deforestation
- Warming ocean currents

Status

 VU Vulnerable

 CR Critically endangered

 EN Endangered

 NT Near threatened

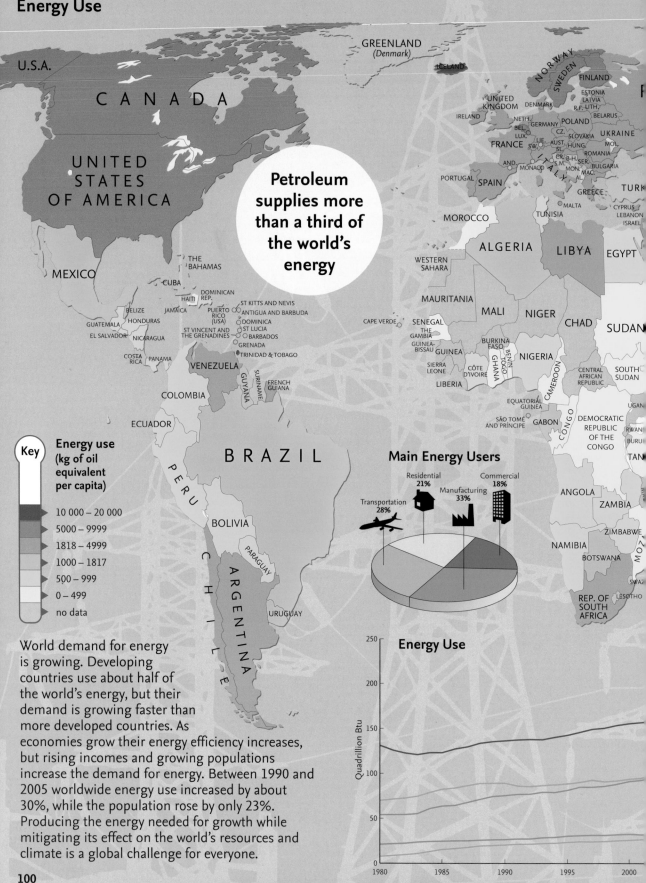

GREENLAND
(Denmark)

ICELAND

U.S.A.

CANADA

NORWAY
SWEDEN
FINLAND

UNITED
KINGDOM
DENMARK
ESTONIA
LATVIA
R.F.
LITH.
BELARUS
IRELAND
NETH.
BEL.
LUX.
GERMANY
POLAND
CZ.
SLOVAKIA
UKRAINE
FRANCE
SW.
LIE.
AUST.
SL.
HUNG.
MOL.
ROMANIA
AND.
CR.
B.H.
SER.
BULGARIA
MONACO
S.M.
MON.
MAC.
AL.
GREECE
TURK
PORTUGAL
SPAIN
ITALY
MALTA
CYPRUS
LEBANON
ISRAEL

UNITED
STATES
OF AMERICA

Petroleum supplies more than a third of the world's energy

MOROCCO
TUNISIA

MEXICO

WESTERN
SAHARA
ALGERIA
LIBYA
EGYPT

THE
BAHAMAS
CUBA
HAITI
DOMINICAN
REP.
JAMAICA
BELIZE
GUATEMALA
HONDURAS
EL SALVADOR
NICARAGUA
ST KITTS AND NEVIS
ANTIGUA AND BARBUDA
PUERTO
RICO
(USA)
DOMINICA
ST LUCIA
ST VINCENT AND
THE GRENADINES
BARBADOS
GRENADA
TRINIDAD & TOBAGO

CAPE VERDE
SENEGAL
THE
GAMBIA
GUINEA-
BISSAU
GUINEA
SIERRA
LEONE
LIBERIA
CÔTE
D'IVOIRE
GHANA
BURKINA
FASO
BENIN
TOGO
NIGERIA

MAURITANIA
MALI
NIGER
CHAD
SUDAN

COSTA
RICA
PANAMA
VENEZUELA
GUYANA
SURINAME
FRENCH
GUIANA

COLOMBIA

ECUADOR

CENTRAL
AFRICAN
REPUBLIC
SOUTH
SUDAN

EQUATORIAL
GUINEA
SÃO TOMÉ
AND PRÍNCIPE
GABON
CONGO
CAMEROON
DEMOCRATIC
REPUBLIC
OF THE
CONGO
UGAN
RWAN
BURU
TAN

PERU

BRAZIL

Key — Energy use (kg of oil equivalent per capita)

- 10 000 – 20 000
- 5000 – 9999
- 1818 – 4999
- 1000 – 1817
- 500 – 999
- 0 – 499
- no data

BOLIVIA

ANGOLA
ZAMBIA

NAMIBIA
ZIMBABWE
BOTSWANA

PARAGUAY

CHILE

ARGENTINA

URUGUAY

REP. OF
SOUTH
AFRICA
LESOTHO
SWAZ

Main Energy Users

Transportation
28%
Residential
21%
Manufacturing
33%
Commercial
18%

World demand for energy is growing. Developing countries use about half of the world's energy, but their demand is growing faster than more developed countries. As economies grow their energy efficiency increases, but rising incomes and growing populations increase the demand for energy. Between 1990 and 2005 worldwide energy use increased by about 30%, while the population rose by only 23%. Producing the energy needed for growth while mitigating its effect on the world's resources and climate is a global challenge for everyone.

Energy Use

Quadrillion Btu

250
200
150
100
50
0

1980   1985   1990   1995   2000

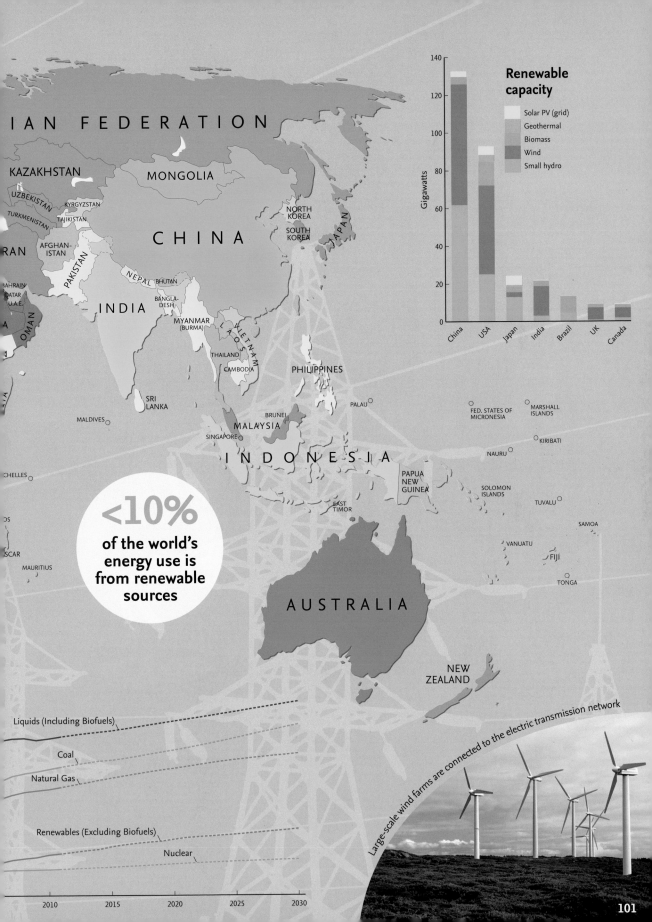

IAN FEDERATION

KAZAKHSTAN

UZBEKISTAN
KYRGYZSTAN
TURKMENISTAN
TAJIKISTAN

IRAN
AFGHAN-
ISTAN

BAHRAIN
QATAR
U.A.E.

OMAN

MONGOLIA

CHINA

NORTH
KOREA

SOUTH
KOREA

JAPAN

PAKISTAN

NEPAL
BHUTAN

BANGLA-
DESH

INDIA

MYANMAR
(BURMA)

LAOS

VIETNAM

THAILAND

CAMBODIA

PHILIPPINES

SRI
LANKA

MALDIVES

BRUNEI

MALAYSIA

SINGAPORE

PALAU

INDONESIA

FED. STATES OF
MICRONESIA

MARSHALL
ISLANDS

KIRIBATI

NAURU

PAPUA
NEW
GUINEA

SOLOMON
ISLANDS

TUVALU

CHELLES

SCAR

MAURITIUS

EAST
TIMOR

SAMOA

VANUATU

FIJI

TONGA

<10%
of the world's
energy use is
from renewable
sources

AUSTRALIA

NEW
ZEALAND

Renewable capacity

- Solar PV (grid)
- Geothermal
- Biomass
- Wind
- Small hydro

Gigawatts

140
120
100
80
60
40
20
0

China USA Japan India Brazil UK Canada

Liquids (Including Biofuels)

Coal

Natural Gas

Renewables (Excluding Biofuels)

Nuclear

2010   2015   2020   2025   2030

Large-scale wind farms are connected to the electric transmission network

101

Primary energy consumption

Primary energy is energy contained in raw fuels. It can be non-renewable or renewable. Non-renewables include the fossil fuels, coal, oil and gas and mineral fuels, eg uranium. Renewables include tidal, solar, wind, geothermal energy and biomass sources.

Values in Tonnes of oil equivalent (toe)

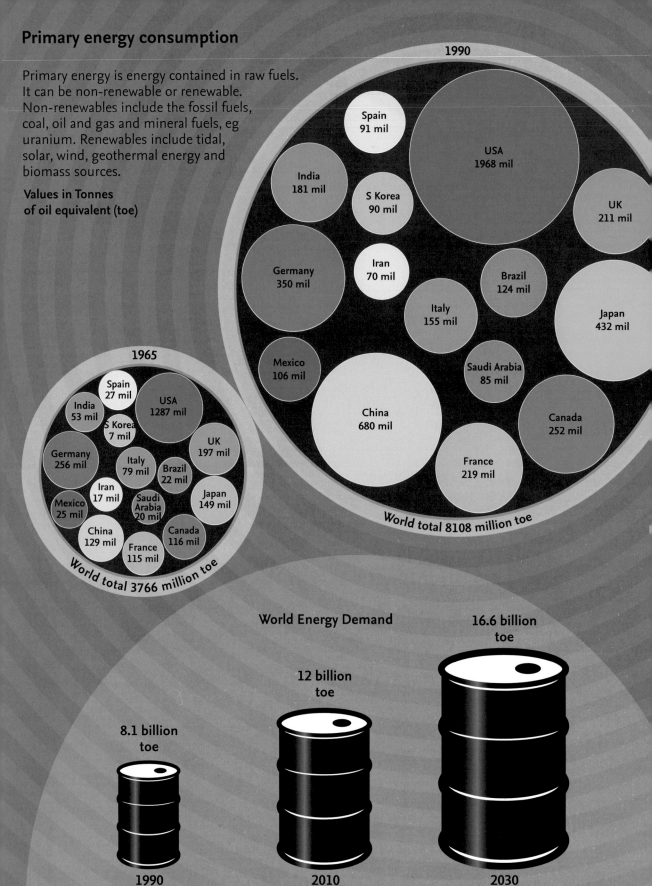

1990

Spain 91 mil

USA 1968 mil

India 181 mil

S Korea 90 mil

UK 211 mil

Germany 350 mil

Iran 70 mil

Brazil 124 mil

Italy 155 mil

Japan 432 mil

Mexico 106 mil

Saudi Arabia 85 mil

China 680 mil

Canada 252 mil

France 219 mil

World total 8108 million toe

1965

Spain 27 mil

India 53 mil

USA 1287 mil

S Korea 7 mil

UK 197 mil

Germany 256 mil

Italy 79 mil

Brazil 22 mil

Iran 17 mil

Japan 149 mil

Mexico 25 mil

Saudi Arabia 20 mil

China 129 mil

France 115 mil

Canada 116 mil

World total 3766 million toe

World Energy Demand

8.1 billion toe

12 billion toe

16.6 billion toe

1990

2010

2030

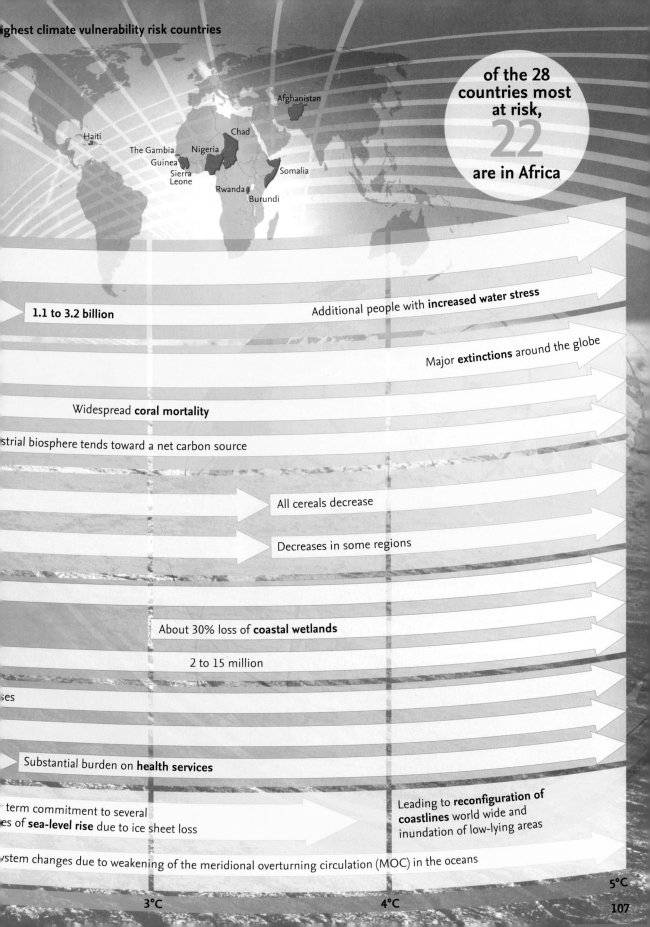

Afghanistan

Haiti

The Gambia
Guinea
Sierra
Leone

Nigeria

Chad

Rwanda

Somalia

Burundi

of the 28 countries most at risk,

22

are in Africa

1.1 to 3.2 billion — Additional people with **increased water stress**

Major **extinctions** around the globe

Widespread **coral mortality**

strial biosphere tends toward a net carbon source

All cereals decrease

Decreases in some regions

About 30% loss of **coastal wetlands**

2 to 15 million

ses

Substantial burden on **health services**

term commitment to several
es of **sea-level rise** due to ice sheet loss

Leading to **reconfiguration of coastlines** world wide and inundation of low-lying areas

stem changes due to weakening of the meridional overturning circulation (MOC) in the oceans

3°C

4°C

5°C

CO₂ Emissions

CO2 emissions (thousands of tonnes)

Algeria 111 304
Argentina 192 378
Australia 399 219
Austria 67 726
Belgium 104 880
Brazil 393 220
Canada 544 091
China 7 031 916
Czech Republic 116 996
Egypt 210 321
France 376 986
Germany 786 660
India 1 742 698
Indonesia 406 029
Iran 538 404
Italy

139 504
960 992

**10 countries
are responsible for**

67%

**of the
world's total CO2
emissions**

6161
48 815
88 202
30 821
91 000
46 908
192 895
780 726
16 054
271 219
120 582
21 404
37 392
109 357

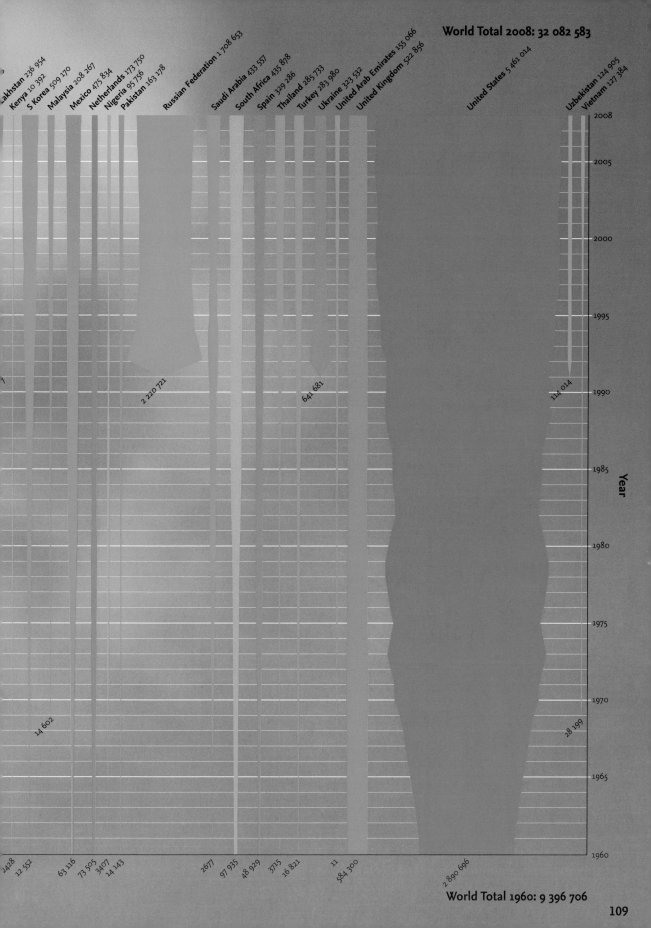

World Total 2008: 32 082 583

...akhstan 236 954
Kenya 10 392
S Korea 509 170
Malaysia 208 267
Mexico 475 834
Netherlands 173 750
Nigeria 95 756
Pakistan 163 178

Russian Federation 1 708 653

Saudi Arabia 433 557
South Africa 435 878
Spain 329 286
Thailand 285 733
Turkey 283 980
Ukraine 323 532
United Arab Emirates 155 066
United Kingdom 522 856

United States 5 461 014

Uzbekistan 124 905
Vietnam 127 384

2008
2005
2000
1995
1990
1985
1980
1975
1970
1965
1960

Year

2 220 721

641 681

114 014

14 602

28 199

2428
12 552
63 116
73 505
3407
14 143
2677
97 935
48 929
3715
16 821
11
584 300
2 890 696

World Total 1960: 9 396 706

109

DEVELOPMENT INDICATORS

Millennium Development Goals

The Millennium Development Goals and targets come from the Millennium Declaration, signed by 189 countries, including 147 heads of state and government, in September 2000 (http://www.un.org/millennium/declaration/ares552e.htm), as updated by the 60th United Nations General Assembly in September 2005. The goals and targets are interrelated and should be seen as a whole. They represent a partnership between the developed countries and the developing countries "to create an environment – at the national and global levels alike – which is conducive to development and the elimination of poverty."

Goal 1 – Eradicate extreme poverty and hunger

1A Halve, between 1990 and 2015, the proportion of people whose income is less than $1 a day

1.1 ▸ Proportion of population below $1 (PPP) per day[1]

1.2 ▸ Poverty gap ratio

1.3 ▸ Share of poorest quintile in national consumption

1B Achieve full and productive employment and decent work for all, including women and young people

1.4 ▸ Growth rate of GDP per person employed

1.5 ▸ Employment-to-population ratio

1.6 ▸ Proportion of employed people living below $1 (PPP) per day

1.7 ▸ Proportion of own-account and contributing family workers in total employment

1C Halve, between 1990 and 2015, the proportion of people who suffer from hunger

1.8 ▸ Prevalence of underweight children under 5 years of age

1.9 ▸ Proportion of population below minimum level of dietary energy consumption

Goal 2 – Achieve universal primary education

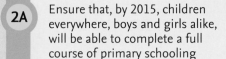

2A Ensure that, by 2015, children everywhere, boys and girls alike, will be able to complete a full course of primary schooling

2.1 ▸ Net enrolment ratio in primary education

2.2 ▸ Proportion of pupils starting grade 1 who reach last grade of primary education

2.3 ▸ Literacy rate of 15–24 year-olds, women and men

Goal 3 – Promote gender equality and empower women

A   Eliminate gender disparity in primary and secondary education, preferably by 2005, and in all levels of education no later than 2015

1   Ratios of girls to boys in primary, secondary, and tertiary education

2   Share of women in wage employment in the non-agricultural sector

3   Proportion of seats held by women in national parliament

Goal 4 – Reduce child mortality

4A   Reduce by two-thirds, between 1990 and 2015, the under-5 mortality rate

4.1   Under-5 mortality rate

4.2   Infant mortality rate

4.3   Proportion of 1-year-old children immunized against measles

Goal 5 – Improve maternal health

A   Reduce by three-quarters, between 1990 and 2015, the maternal mortality ratio

1   Maternal mortality ratio

2   Proportion of births attended by skilled health personnel

5B   Achieve, by 2015, universal access to reproductive health

5.3   Contraceptive prevalence rate

5.4   Adolescent birth rate

5.5   Antenatal care coverage (at least one visit and at least four visits)

5.6   Unmet need for family planning

Goal 6 – Combat HIV/AIDS, malaria, and other diseases

A   Have halted by 2015 and begun to reverse the spread of HIV/AIDS

1   HIV prevalence among population aged 15–24 years

2   Condom use at last high-risk sex

3   Proportion of population aged 15–24 years with comprehensive correct knowledge of HIV/AIDS

4   Ratio of school attendance of orphans to school attendance of nonorphans aged 10–14 years

B   Achieve, by 2010, universal access to treatment for HIV/AIDS for all those who need it

5   Proportion of population with advanced HIV infection with access to antiretroviral drugs

6C   Have halted by 2015 and begun to reverse the incidence of malaria and other major diseases

6.6   Incidence and death rates associated with malaria

6.7   Proportion of children under-5 sleeping under insecticide-treated bednets

6.8   Proportion of children under-5 with fever who are treated with appropriate anti-malarial drugs

6.9   Incidence, prevalence, and death rates associated with tuberculosis

6.10   Proportion of tuberculosis cases detected and cured under directly observed treatment short course

Millennium Development Goals

Goal 7 – Ensure environmental sustainability

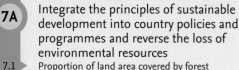

7A Integrate the principles of sustainable development into country policies and programmes and reverse the loss of environmental resources

7.1 ▸ Proportion of land area covered by forest

7.2 ▸ CO_2 emissions, total, per capita and per \$1 GDP (PPP)

7.3 ▸ Consumption of ozone-depleting substances

7.4 ▸ Proportion of fish stocks within safe biological limits

7.5 ▸ Proportion of total water resources used

7B Reduce biodiversity loss, achieving, by 2010, a significant reduction in the rate of loss

7.6 ▸ Proportion of terrestrial and marine areas protected

7.7 ▸ Proportion of species threatened with extinction

7C Halve, by 2015, the proportion of people without sustainable access to safe drinking water and basic sanitation

7.8 ▸ Proportion of population using an improved drinking water source

7.9 ▸ Proportion of population using an improved sanitation facility

7D By 2020, achieve a significant improvement in the lives of at least 100 million slum dwellers

7.10 ▸ Proportion of urban population living in slums [2]

The Millennium Development Goals are ends in themselves, but they are also the means to a productive life, to economic growth, and to further development. A healthier worker is a more productive worker. A better educated worker is a more productive worker.

United Nations
Development Programme
www.undp.org

Goal 8 – Develop a global partnership for development

A
Develop further an open, rule-based, predictable, non-discriminatory trading and financial system

Includes a commitment to good governance, development, and poverty reduction—both nationally and internationally

B
Address the special needs of the least-developed countries

Includes: tariff and quota-free access for the least-developed countries' exports; enhanced programme of debt relief for heavily indebted poor countries (HIPC) and cancellation of official bilateral debt; and more generous official development assistance (ODA) for countries committed to poverty reduction

C
Address the special needs of landlocked developing countries and small island developing states (through the Programme of Action for the Sustainable Development of Small Island Developing States and the outcome of the 22nd special session of the General Assembly)

D
Deal comprehensively with the debt problems of developing countries through national and international measures in order to make debt sustainable in the long term

---

Some of the indicators listed below are monitored separately for the least developed countries (LDCs), Africa, landlocked developing countries, and small island developing states.

Official development assistance (ODA)

8.1 ▸ Net ODA, total and to the least developed countries, as percentage of OECD/DAC donors' gross national income

8.2 ▸ Proportion of total bilateral, sector-allocable ODA of OECD/DAC donors to basic social services (basic education, primary health care, nutrition, safe water and sanitation)

8.3 ▸ Proportion of bilateral official development assistance of OECD/DAC donors that is untied

8.4 ▸ ODA received in landlocked developing countries as a proportion of their gross national incomes

8.5 ▸ ODA received in small island developing states as a proportion of their gross national incomes

Market access

8.6 ▸ Proportion of total developed country imports (by value and excluding arms) from developing countries and least developed countries, admitted free of duty

8.7 ▸ Average tariffs imposed by developed countries on agricultural products and textiles and clothing from developing countries

8.8 ▸ Agricultural support estimate for OECD countries as a percentage of their gross domestic product

8.9 ▸ Proportion of ODA provided to help build trade capacity

Debt sustainability

8.10 ▸ Total number of countries that have reached their HIPC decision points and number that have reached their HIPC completion points (cumulative)

8.11 ▸ Debt relief committed under HIPC and MDRI Initiatives

8.12 ▸ Debt service as a percentage of exports of goods and services

---

E
In cooperation with pharmaceutical companies, provide access to affordable essential drugs in developing countries

8.13 ▸ Proportion of population with access to affordable essential drugs on a sustainable basis

8F
In cooperation with the private sector, make available the benefits of new technologies, especially information and communications

8.14 ▸ Telephone lines per 100 population

8.15 ▸ Cellular subscribers per 100 population

8.16 ▸ Internet users per 100 population

---

indicators should be disaggregated by sex and urban/rural location as far as possible.

r monitoring country poverty trends, indicators based on national poverty lines should be used, where available.

e actual proportion of people living in slums is measured by a proxy, represented by the urban population living in seholds with at least one of the four characteristics: (a) lack of access to improved water supply; (b) lack of access to roved sanitation; (c) overcrowding (3 or more persons per room); and (d) dwellings made of non-durable material.

Millennium Development Goals 2010 Indicators

	World	High income	East Asia & Pacific	Europe & Central Asia	Latin America & Caribbean	Middle East & North Africa	South Asia	Sub-Saharan Africa
Goal 1 – Eradicate extreme poverty and hunger								
Employment to population ratio, 15+, total (%)	61	56	68	53	60	47	56	65
Employment to population ratio, ages 15-24, total (%)	45	40	51	35	44	29	42	49
GDP per person (annual % growth)	3	2	6	2	5	2	7	2
Income share held by lowest 20%	..	..	..	4	..	..	..	..
Malnutrition prevalence, weight for age (% of children under 5)	21.4	..	12.9	..	3.8	6.6	42.5	24.6
Poverty gap at $1.25 a day (PPP) (%)	..	..	..	..	..	..	8.6	..
Poverty headcount ratio at $1.25 a day (PPP) (% of population)	..	..	17	..	8	4	36	51
Prevalence of undernourishment (% of population)	13	5	11	6	9	7	20	22
Vulnerable employment, total (% of total employment)	..	..	..	14	30	37	..	..
Goal 2 – Achieve universal primary education								
Literacy rate, youth female (% ages 15-24)	87	99+	98	99	97	86	72	67
Literacy rate, youth male (% ages 15-24)	92	99+	98	99	97	93	85	77
Persistence to last grade of primary, total (% of cohort)	..	..	..	97	81	85	..	..
Primary completion rate, total (% of relevant age group)	86	97	100	97	101	88	86	67
Total enrolment, primary (% net)	90	96	94	94	95	92	91	74
Goal 3 – Promote gender equality and empower women								
Proportion of seats held by women in national parliaments (%)	20	23	18	22	23	9	20	20
Ratio of female to male enrolments in tertiary education	108	123	104	124	128	101	69	63
Ratio of female to male primary enrolment	96	100	101	99	97	93	95	92
Ratio of female to male secondary enrolment	97	99	105	98	108	93	88	79
Share of women employed in the nonagricultural sector (% of total nonagricultural employment)	36.6	47	39.3	47.8	40.4	19.6	18	..
Goal 4 – Reduce child mortality								
Immunization, measles (% of children ages 12-23 months)	85	93	95	95	93	90	77	76
Mortality rate, infant (per 1000 live births)	41	5	19	12	18	26	52	76
Mortality rate, under-5 (per 1000)	58	6	23	14	23	31	67	121
Goal 5 – Improve maternal health								
Adolescent fertility rate (births per 1000 women ages 15-19)	54	19	18	20	72	36	75	110
Births attended by skilled health staff (% of total)	65	99	89	95	90	81	47	44
Contraceptive prevalence (% of women ages 15-49)	61	..	76	..	74.7	60	51	21
Maternal mortality ratio (per 100 000 live births)	400	10	150	45	130	200	500	900
Pregnant women receiving prenatal care (%)	82	..	91	..	95	83	70	71
Unmet need for contraception (% of married women ages 15-49)	..	..	..	..	..	..	15	24

	World	High income	East Asia & Pacific	Europe & Central Asia	Latin America & Caribbean	Middle East & North Africa	South Asia	Sub-Saharan Africa
Goal 6 – Combat HIV/AIDS, malaria, and other diseases								
Children with fever receiving antimalarial drugs (% of children under age 5 with fever)	..	..	..	..	..	..	7	35
Condom use, female (% ages 15-24)	..	..	..	..	..	..	6	19
Condom use, male (% ages 15-24)	..	..	..	..	..	..	15	36
Incidence of tuberculosis (per 100 000 people)	128	14	114	46	43	38	192	271
Prevalence of HIV, female (% ages 15-24)	0.7	0.1	0.2	0.2	0.4	..	0.1	3.8
Prevalence of HIV, male (% ages 15-24)	0.4	0.2	0	0.1	1	..	0.1	1.5
Prevalence of HIV, total (% of population ages 15-49)	0.8	0.3	0.2	0.4	0.5	0.1	0.3	5.5
Tuberculosis case detection rate (%, all forms)	65	85	77	74	80	74	58	60
Goal 7 – Ensure environmental sustainability								
CO_2 emissions (kg per PPP $ of GDP)	0.4	0.3	0.6	0.3	0.3	0.6	0.5	0.4
CO_2 emissions (metric tons per capita)	4.8	11.9	5.0	7.9	2.9	5.6	1.3	0.8
Forest area (% of land area)	31	29	27	38	47	2	17	28
Improved sanitation facilities (% of population with access)	61	100	63	94	79	85	36	31
Improved water source (% of population with access)	87	100	89	98	93	88	87	60
Marine protected areas, (% of territorial waters)	9.2	15.1	11	9.1	13	2.2	1.7	4.7
Terrestrial protected areas (% of total land area)	12.5	13.4	14	9.2	20.8	9.2	6.1	11.7
Goal 8 – Develop a global partnership for development								
Debt service (PPG and IMF only, % of exports, excluding workers' remittances)	..	..	1	4	6	9	2.8	2.7
Internet users (per 100 people)	30.5	75.1	35.6	56.7	34	25	8.4	10.9
Mobile cellular subscriptions (per 100 people)	79	110	76.6	122.7	98	97	61	44.7
Net ODA received per capita (current US$)	19	0.4	5	13	16	37	9	54
Telephone lines (per 100 people)	17	44	21.5	36	18	17	3	1
Other								
Fertility rate, total (births per woman)	2.5	1.7	1.8	1.7	2.3	2.7	2.8	5
GNI per capita, Atlas method (current US$)	9136	38696	7118	23335	7891	6378	1216	1187
GNI, Atlas method (current US$ billions)	62492.5	43610	15670	20773	4647	2394	1920	1013.9
Gross capital formation (% of GDP)	19.8	17.9	25.5	18.8	21.7	24.9	31.5	23.7
Life expectancy at birth, total (years)	69	79	73	75	73	72	65	54
Literacy rate, adult total (% of people ages 15 and above)	84	98	93	98	91	73	61	62
Population, total (millions)	6840.5	1127	2202	8902	589	382.8	1579.5	854.3
Trade (% of GDP)	55.9	55.8	63	77.8	44.7	85.5	45.0	61.8

.. Not available.
Figures in italics are for an earlier year.
Source: World Development Indicators Database

Millennium Development Goals Achievement Fund

The Millennium Development Goals Achievement Fund was established in 2006, to support national governments, local authorities and citizen organizations in their efforts to tackle poverty and inequality.

Guatemala (5)
$29 749 000

Bolivia (4)
$28 000 000

China (4)
$30 600 000

Ethiopia (5)
$26 499 906

Nicaragua (6)
$39 274 000

Colombia (4)
$25 699 884

Mauritania (4)
$25 000 000

Bosnia and Herzegovina (4)
$23 948 728

Philippines (4)
$22 875 000

Ecuador (4)
$20 976 900

Honduras (3)
$20 872 000

130 programmes in 50 countries spread across 5 regions of the world are helping more than

3.5

million people

Brazil (
$16 020

Panama (4)
$20 500 000

Mozambique (3)
$17 500 000

Turkey (4)
$17 478 478

Costa Rica (4)
$16 516 000

El Salvador (3)
$18 198 879

Peru (4)
$17 925 001

Afghanistan
$16 500 000

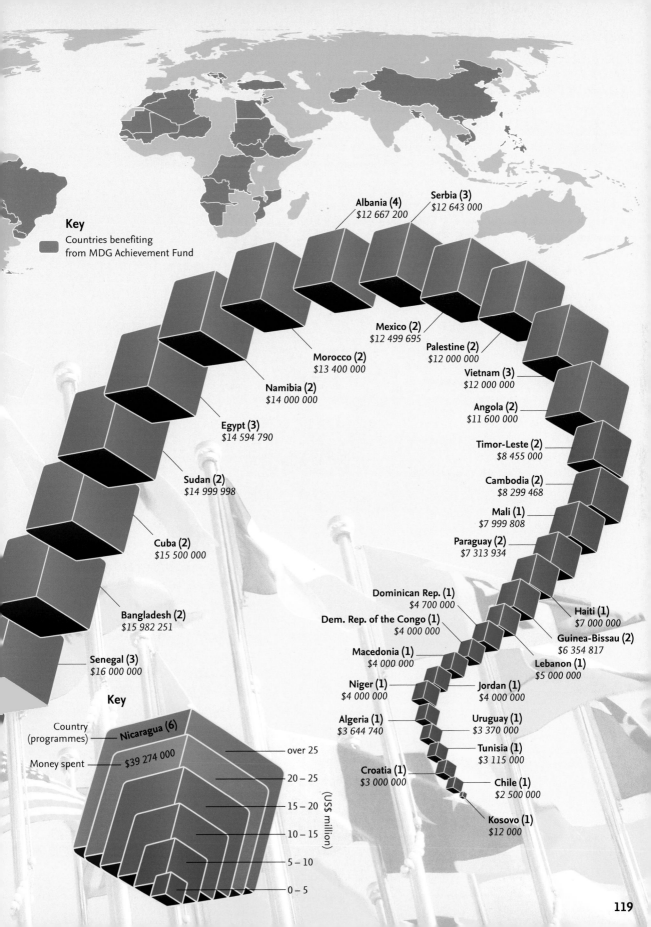

Key

Countries benefiting
from MDG Achievement Fund

Albania (4)
$12 667 200

Serbia (3)
$12 643 000

Mexico (2)
$12 499 695

Palestine (2)
$12 000 000

Morocco (2)
$13 400 000

Vietnam (3)
$12 000 000

Namibia (2)
$14 000 000

Angola (2)
$11 600 000

Egypt (3)
$14 594 790

Timor-Leste (2)
$8 455 000

Sudan (2)
$14 999 998

Cambodia (2)
$8 299 468

Mali (1)
$7 999 808

Cuba (2)
$15 500 000

Paraguay (2)
$7 313 934

Dominican Rep. (1)
$4 700 000

Haiti (1)
$7 000 000

Dem. Rep. of the Congo (1)
$4 000 000

Guinea-Bissau (2)
$6 354 817

Macedonia (1)
$4 000 000

Lebanon (1)
$5 000 000

Bangladesh (2)
$15 982 251

Niger (1)
$4 000 000

Jordan (1)
$4 000 000

Senegal (3)
$16 000 000

Algeria (1)
$3 644 740

Uruguay (1)
$3 370 000

Tunisia (1)
$3 115 000

Croatia (1)
$3 000 000

Chile (1)
$2 500 000

Kosovo (1)
$12 000

Key

Country
(programmes)

Money spent

Nicaragua (6)

$39 274 000

over 25

20 – 25

15 – 20

10 – 15

(US$ million)

5 – 10

0 – 5

World Statistics

	Total population 2011	Life expectancy at birth 2009	Under 5 mortality rate per 1000 live births 2010	Improved water source % population with access 2008	Adult literacy % population over 15 years 2009	Primary school enrolment % net 2008/2009
Afghanistan	32 358 000	44	103	48	..	..
Albania	3 216 000	77	16	97	96	85
Algeria	35 980 000	73	31	83	73	94
Andorra	86 000	..	3	100	..	82
Angola	19 618 000	48	98	50	70	..
Antigua and Barbuda	90 000	..	7	91	99	88
Argentina	40 765 000	76	12	97	98	..
Armenia	3 100 000	74	18	96	100	..
Australia	22 606 000	82	4	100	..	97
Austria	8 413 000	80	4	100	..	..
Azerbaijan	9 306 000	70	39	80	100	85
Bahamas, The	347 000	74	14	97	..	91
Bahrain	1 324 000	76	9	..	91	97
Bangladesh	150 494 000	67	38	80	56	86
Barbados	274 000	77	17	100	..	..
Belarus	9 559 000	70	4	100	100	94
Belgium	10 754 000	81	4	100	..	99
Belize	318 000	77	14	99	..	97
Benin	9 100 000	62	73	75	42	92
Bhutan	738 000	67	44	92	53	87
Bolivia	10 088 000	66	42	86	91	..
Bosnia-Herzegovina	3 752 000	75	8	99	98	87
Botswana	2 031 000	55	36	95	84	..
Brazil	196 655 000	73	17	97	90	95
Brunei	406 000	78	6	99	95	93
Bulgaria	7 446 000	73	11	100	98	97

GNI per capita US$ 2010	Mobile cellular subscriptions per 100 people 2010	Aid per capita US$ 2009	Forest area % of total land area 2010	Nationally protected area % of total land area 2009	CO_2 emissions per capita tonnes 2007	
7 760	121	5	62	18	7	Malaysia
4 240	157	108	3	..	3	Maldives
600	48	76	10	2	0	Mali
18 430	109	..	1	17	7	Malta
3 450	7	963	72	3	2	Marshall Islands
1 030	79	87	0	1	1	Mauritania
7 750	92	122	17	4	3	Mauritius
8 930	81	2	33	11	4	Mexico
2 700	25	1 093	91	4	1	Fed. States of Micronesia
1 810	89	68	12	1	1	Moldova
183 150	74	..	0	24	..	Monaco
1 850	91	139	7	13	4	Mongolia
6 620	185	121	40	13	..	Montenegro
2 900	100	29	11	2	1	Morocco
440	31	88	50	16	0	Mozambique
..	1	7	49	6	0	Myanmar
4 500	67	150	9	14	1	Namibia
480	31	29	25	17	0	Nepal
49 750	116	..	11	12	11	Netherlands
29 050	115	..	31	26	8	New Zealand
1 090	65	135	26	37	1	Nicaragua
370	25	31	1	7	0	Niger
1 180	55	11	10	13	1	Nigeria
..	2	3	47	4	3	North Korea
85 340	113	..	33	14	9	Norway
18 260	166	75	0	11	15	Oman

World Statistics

	Total population 2011	Life expectancy at birth 2009	Under 5 mortality rate per 1000 live births 2010	Improved water source % population with access 2008	Adult literacy % population over 15 years 2009	Primary school enrolment % net 2008/2009
Pakistan	176 745 000	67	70	90	56	66
Palau	21 000	..	15	84	..	..
Panama	3 571 000	76	17	93	94	97
Papua New Guinea	7 014 000	61	47	40	60	..
Paraguay	6 568 000	72	21	86	95	85
Peru	29 400 000	74	15	82	90	94
Philippines	94 852 000	72	23	91	95	92
Poland	38 299 000	76	5	100	100	96
Portugal	10 690 000	79	3	99	95	99
Puerto Rico	3 746 000	..	..	..	..	..
Qatar	1 870 000	76	7	100	95	93
Romania	21 436 000	73	11	..	98	90
Russian Federation	142 836 000	69	9	96	100	92
Rwanda	10 943 000	51	59	65	71	96
St. Kitts and Nevis	53 000	..	7	99	..	91
St. Lucia	176 000	..	14	98	..	91
St. Vincent & the Grenadines	109 000	72	19	..	..	95
Samoa	184 000	72	17	88	99	90
San Marino	32 000	83	2	..	..	92
São Tomé and Príncipe	169 000	66	53	89	89	97
Saudi Arabia	28 083 000	73	15	96	86	86
Senegal	12 768 000	56	50	69	50	73
Serbia	7 307 000	74	6	99	..	94
Seychelles	87 000	74	12	..	92	94
Sierra Leone	5 997 000	48	114	49	41	..
Singapore	5 188 000	81	2	100	95	..

pulation, average annual growth rate The exponential rate of change in population for the period indicated. (World Bank)

pulation, total Midyear population that includes all residents regardless of legal status or citizenship – except for refugees not permanently settled in the country of asylum, who are generally considered part of the population of their country of origin. (World Bank)

pulation below $1.25 per day The proportion of the population living on less than $1.25 a day at 2005 purchasing power parity prices. (World Bank)

pulation below $2 per day The proportion of the population living on less than $2 a day at 2005 purchasing power parity prices. (World Bank)

pulation density Midyear population divided by land area in square kilometres. (World Bank)

pulation, rural Calculated as the difference between the total population and the urban population. (World Bank)

pulation, urban The midyear population of areas defined as urban in each country and reported to the United Nations. (UN World Urbanization Prospects, The 2011 Revision, and World Bank staff estimates)

egnant women receiving prenatal care The proportion of women attended at least once during pregnancy by skilled health personnel for reasons related to pregnancy. (Household Surveys)

rchasing power parity (PPP) conversion factor The number of units of a country's currency required to buy the same amount of goods and services in the domestic market as a U.S. dollar would buy in the United States. (World Bank)

fugees People recognized as refugees under the 1951 Convention Relating to the Status of Refugees or its 1967 Protocol; the 1969 Organization of African Unity Convention Governing the Specific Aspects of Refugee Problems in Africa; people recognised as refugees in accordance with the UNHCR statute; people granted a refugee-like humanitarian status; and people provided with temporary protection. Palestinian refugees (and their descendants) are people whose residence was Palestine between June 1946 and May 1948, and who lost their homes and means of livelihood as a result of the 1948 Arab-Israeli conflict. (UNHCR and UNRWA)

Services Economic activity corresponding to International Standard Industrial Classification (ISIC) divisions 6–9 (ISIC revision 2) or tabulation categories G–P (ISIC revision 3). (ILO)

Trade Refers to the two-way flow of exports and imports of goods (merchandise trade) and services (service trade).

Tuberculosis, incidence of The estimated number of new pulmonary, smear-positive, and extrapulmonary tuberculosis cases. (WHO)

Undernourishment, prevalence of The percentage of the population that is undernourished – whose dietary energy consumption is continuously below a minimum dietary energy requirement for maintaining a healthy life and carrying out light physical activity. (FAO)

Water source, access to an improved The share of the population with reasonable access to an adequate amount of water from an improved source, such as a household connection, public standpipe, borehole, protected well or spring, or rainwater collection. Unimproved sources include vendors, tanker trucks, and unprotected wells and springs. Reasonable access is defined as the availability of at least 20 litres a person per day from a source within one kilometre of the dwelling. (WHO and UNICEF)

World Bank Atlas method A conversion factor to convert national currency units to U.S. dollars at prevailing exchange rates, adjusted for inflation and averaged over three years. The purpose is to reduce the effect of exchange rate fluctuations in the cross-country comparison of national incomes. (World Bank)

Notes

Data sources

The indicators presented in this book are compiled by international agencies and by public and private organizations, usually on the basis of survey data or administrative statistics obtained from national governments. The principal source of each indicator is given in parentheses following the definition.

Abbreviations

CDIAC	Carbon Dioxide Information Analysis Center	UCW	Understanding Children's Work
DAC	Development Assistance Committee of the Organization for Economic Co-operation and Development	UN	United Nations
		UNAIDS	Joint United Nations Programme on HIV/AID
FAO	Food and Agriculture Organization of the United Nations	UNDP	United Nations Development Programme
		UNEP	United Nations Environment Programme
GDP	Gross Domestic Product	UNESCO	United Nations Educational, Scientific and Cultural Organization
GNI	Gross National Income		
HIPC	Heavily Indebted Poor Countries	UNFPA	United Nations Population Fund
ICT	Information and Communications Technology	UNHCR	United Nations High Commissioner for Refugees
IDA	International Development Association		
IEA	International Energy Agency	UNICEF	United Nations Children's Fund
ILO	International Labour Organization	UNPD	United Nations Procurement Division
IMF	International Monetary Fund	UNRWA	United Nations Relief and Works Agency
ITU	International Telecommunication Union	UNSD	United Nations Statistics Division
MDGs	Millennium Development Goals	WCMC	World Conservation Monitoring Centre
OECD	Organization for Economic Co-operation and Development	WDI	World Development Indicators
		WHO	World Health Organization
PPP	Purchasing Power Parity	WRI	World Resources Institute
		WTO	World Trade Organization

For more information

- *World Development Indicators* and **WDI Online** are the World Bank's premier compilation of data about development. This *Atlas* complements *World Development Indicators* by providing a geographical view of pertinent data. The *World Development Indicators* is available at: www.worldbank.org/data/wdi

- *Global Development Finance* and **GDF Online** are the World Bank's comprehensive compilation of data on external debt and financial flows. They are available at: www.worldbank.org/data/gdf

- *African Development Indicators*, the World Bank's most detailed collection of data on Africa, available in one volume at: www.worldbank.org/adi

- **The Millennium Development Goals** (MDG) and the data and indicators required to track progress toward them are available at: www.developmentgoals.org

- **The PARIS21 Consortium** and information about how it promotes evidence-based policymaking and monitoring are available at: www.paris21.org

- **The Statistical Capacity Building Program**, which offers tools and advice for statistical capacity building in developing countries, can be accessed at: www.worldbank.org/data/statcap

- **The International Comparison Program** (ICP) and information about the ICP and the final results from the 2005 round can be found at: www.worldbank.org/data/icp

- **Indicate**, a brand new statistical analysis tool allowing you to explore the most up-to-date authoritative statistics. A demo is available online at: www.collinsindicate.com

Index

Acknowledgements

Photo credits

Shutterstock: pp8-9 newart, pp12-13 Aleksandar Videnovic, p13 Manfred Steinbach, pp14-15 Vaju Ariel, p14 SFC, pp16-17 Albert Campbell, p16 Hector Conesa, p17 Francis Wong Chee Yen, p18 Timothy Large, p19 Lucian Coman, pp20-21 arbit, p20 Andresr, p21 John Steel, pp22-23 newart, p22 Suat Gürsözlü, p24 (Los Angeles) Linda Armstrong, p24 (New York) akva, p24 (Mexico City) Frontpage, p24 (São Paulo) jbor, p25 (Moscow) Sergey Skleznev, p25 (Tokyo) J. Henning Buchholz, p25 (Cairo) DUMITRU, p25 (Shanghai) Mateo_Pearson, p25 (Kolkata) JeremyRichards, p25 (Karachi) Pichugin Dmitry, p25 (Mumbai) Alfredo Ragazzoni, pp26-27 Robert Adrian Hillman, pp28-29 atanas.dk, p29 Richard Thornton, p32 Monkey Business Images, pp36-37 Oxlock, p36 Lucian Coman, p37(bottom right) Sebastian Kaulitzki, p37 (centre right) Miguel Angel Salinas Salinas, pp38-39 CarpathianPrince, pp38-39 Nataliia Natykach, pp38-39 Artix Studio, pp38-39 ESW, pp38-39 Dragana Gerasimoski, pp38-39 Athanasia Nomikou, pp38-39 Z-art, pp38-39 Miguel Angel Salinas Salinas, p41 Stuart Monk, pp44-45 Andrey Armyagov, p44 (hamburger) Robert Forrest, p44 (glass of milk) vikhr, p44 (egg) Sergey Titov, p44 (orange) ElenaShow, p44 (potato) Oleksii Natykach, p44 (tomato) Robert Forrest, p45 Chris Bence, pp46-47 Oksana Petrova, p47 thefinalmiracle, p47 (bottom) KamiGami, pp48-49 williammpark, pp48-49 Sebastian Kaulitzki, pp48-49 DVARG, pp48-49 Alila Sao Mai, pp52-53 AridOcean, pp52-53 Alila Sao Mai, pp52-53 Sebastian Kaulitzki, p55 (left) olly, p55 (right) CarpathianPrince, pp58-59 crop, p58 elwynn, p59 deMatos, pp62-63 ifong, pp62-63 Rey Kamensky, p63 vectomart, p73 TebNad, pp80-81 Nataliia Natykach, p82 Mikhail Markovskiy, p83 Peter Zaharov, p83 NASA's Earth Observatory, pp84-85 Jezper, pp84-85 Nataliia Natykach, p87 (top) Barnaby Chambers, p87 (bottom) Petr Vopenka, pp88-89 Binkski, p88 Antonio V. Oquias, pp90-91 newphotoservice, pp92-93 chinahbzyg, p94 (polar bear) Steffen Foerster Photography, p94 (turtle) Lui, Tat Mun, p94 (tiger) mlorenz, p94 (panda) Regien Paassen, p95 imigra, pp96-97 mika48, pp98-99 Chuck Rausin, p98 (polar bear) Wild Arctic Pictures, p98 (elephants) Ekkachai, p98 (tuna) holbox, p98 (gorilla) PRILL Mediendesign und Fotografie, p98 (panda) Regien Paassen, p99 (turtle) Lui, Tat Mun, p99 (tiger) Tiago Jorge da Silva Estima, p99 (macaw) poeticpenguin, p99 (penguin) Yevgenia Gorbulsky, pp100-101 Fedorov Oleksiy, p101 Dmitriy Yakovlev, p102 astudio, p105 Christopher Wood, pp106-107 Prokhorova Nadiia, pp106-107 Nejron Photo, pp108-109 Robert Adrian Hillman, p112 Lucian Coman, p114 PBorowka, pp118-119 velirina, pp118-119 doodle.

Still Pictures: p65 McPHOTO, pp68-69 Ron Giling/Lineair, p71 sinopictures/CNS, p75 JOERG BOETHLING.

World Bank/Ami Vitale: p34